i Think: it's Elementary!

America's Colonies

by Kendra Corr

© InspirEd Educators, Inc.   Atlanta, Georgia

** It is the goal of InspirEd Educators to create instructional materials that are interesting, engaging, and challenging. Our student-centered approach incorporates both content and skills, placing particular emphasis on reading, writing, vocabulary development, and critical and creative thinking in the content areas.

Edited by Sharon Coletti and Amy Hellen

Cover graphics by Sharon Coletti and Print1 Direct

Copyright © 2010 by InspirEd Educators, Inc.

ISBN # 978-1-933558-83-7

Printed in the United States of America

About InspirEd Educators

InspirEd Educators was founded in 2000 by author Sharon Coletti. Our mission is to provide interesting, student-centered, and thought-provoking instructional materials. To accomplish this, we design lesson plans with standards-based content presented in a variety of ways and used as the vehicle for developing critical and creative thinking, reading, writing, collaboration, problem-solving, and other necessary and enduring skills. By requiring students to THINK, our lessons ensure FAR greater retention than simple memorization of facts!

Initially our company offered large, comprehensive, multi-disciplinary social studies curricula. Then in 2008 we joined forces with another small company and author, Kendra Corr, and launched a second line of thematic units, some excerpted and adapted from our original products. These flexible and affordable resources are ideal for individual, small, or large-group instruction. We hope you will find our company's unique approach valuable and that we can serve you again in the near future.

If you are interested in our other offerings, you can find information on our website at **www.inspirededucators.com**.

InspirEd Educators materials provide engaging lesson plans that vary daily and include:

- Lesson-specific Springboards (warm-ups)
- Writing activities
- Critical and creative thinking
- Problem-solving
- Test-taking skill development
- Primary source analyses (DBQ's)
- Multiple perspectives
- Graphic analyses
- Fascinating readings
- Simulations
- Story-telling
- Practical use of technology
- Debates
- Plays
- Research
- Graphic organizers
- AND SO MUCH MORE!!!!!

Thank you for choosing our units,
Sharon Coletti, President
InspirEd Educators

Tips for Teaching with this InspirEd Unit

- Before beginning the unit, take time to look through the Objectives and lessons. This will give you a chance to think about what you want to emphasize and decide upon any modifications, connections, or extensions you'd like to include.

- Arrange for your student(s) to have books available or to check them out. A suggested reading list is included, but any books of interest related to the unit subject are fine. We do strongly suggest the reading link to enhance this study! Activities are included that refer to the book(s) being read, and students should be encouraged to discuss any connections throughout.

- Give your student(s) a copy of the Objective page at the beginning of unit study. The Objectives serve as an outline of the content to be covered and provide a means to review information. Have the student(s) define the vocabulary terms as they progress through the lessons and thoroughly answer the essential questions. You can review their responses as you go along or wait and check everything as a test review. It is important that your student(s) have some opportunity to receive feedback on their Objective answers, since assessments provided at the end of the unit are based on these.

- Read through each lesson's materials before beginning. This will help you better understand lesson concepts; decide when and how to present the vocabulary and prepare the handouts (or transparencies) you will need.

- "Terms to know" can be introduced at the beginning of lessons or reviewed at the end, unless specified otherwise. (In a few instances the intent is for students to discover the meanings of the terms.)

- Our materials are intended to prompt discussion. Often students' answers may vary, but it's important that they be able to substantiate their opinions and ideas with facts. Let the discussion flow!

- Note that differentiated assessments are provided at the end of the unit. Feel free to use any of these as appropriate; cut-and-paste to revise, or create your own tests as desired.

- For additional information and research sites refer to the Resource Section in the back of the unit.

- InspirEd Educators units are all about thinking and creativity, so allow yourself the freedom to adapt the materials as you see fit. Our goal is to provide a springboard for you to jump from in your teaching and your student(s)' learning.

- ENJOY! We at InspirEd Educators truly believe that teaching and learning should be enjoyable, so we do our best to make our lessons interesting and varied. We want you and your student(s) to love learning!

Table of Contents

 # Some Suggested Reading

NOTE: Depending upon ability, have your student(s) read one or more of the following titles (or others as available) on the topic of the American Colonies to accompany this unit study. The final lesson pertains to the chosen book(s).

Benge, Geoff, and Benge, Janet, <u>John Smith: A Foothold in the New World</u>, Emerald Books, 2006.

* Bulla, Clyde Robert, <u>Charlie's House</u>, Knopf, 1993.

* Bulla, Clyde Robert, <u>A Lion to Guard Us</u>, Harper Collins, 1981.

Bulla, Clyde Robert, <u>Pocahontas and the Strangers,</u> Crowell, 1971.

Bulla, Clyde Robert, <u>Squanto, a Friend of the Pilgrims</u>, Scholastic Paperbacks, 1990.

** Carbone, Elisa, <u>Blood on the River: James Town 1607</u>, Puffin, 2007.

Clapp, Patricia, <u>Constance: A Story of Early Plymouth</u>, Morrow, 1968.

Clapp, Patricia, <u>Witches' Children: A Story of Salem</u>, Puffin, 1987.

* Dalgliesh, Alice, <u>The Courage of Sarah Noble</u>, Aladdin, 1991.

Dillon, Eilis, <u>The Seekers</u>, Puffin, 1987.

* Edmonds, Walter D., <u>The Matchlock Gun</u>, Putnam Juvenile, 1988.

** Field, Rachel, <u>Calico Bush</u>, Aladdin, 1998.

Fleischman, Paul, <u>Saturnalia,</u> Harper Collins, 1990.

Hermes, Patricia, <u>My America: Our Strange New Land, Elizabeth's Jamestown Colony Diary, Book One</u>, Scholastic, 2002.

Hermes, Patricia, <u>The Starving Time: Elizabeth's Diary, Book Two, Jamestown, Virginia, 1609</u>, Scholastic, 2002.

Jackson, Dave, <u>The Mayflower Secret: William Bradford</u> (Trailblazer Books #26) Bethany House, 1998.

Jackson, Dave and Jackson, Netta, <u>Hostage on the Nighthawk: William Penn</u> (Trailblazer Books #32), Bethany Books, 2000.

Karwoski, Gail, <u>Surviving Jamestown: The Adventures of Young Sam Collier</u>, Peachtree Publishers, 2001.

Keehn, Sally M., <u>I Am Regina</u>, Putnam Juvenile, 2001.

Koller, Jackie French, <u>The Primrose Way</u>, Harcourt, 1992.

Lasky, Kathryn, <u>A Journey to the New World: The Diary of Remember Patience Whipple, Mayflower, 1620,</u> Scholastic, 1996.

O'Dell, Scott, <u>Serpent Never Sleeps</u>, Fawcett, 1988.

Osborne, Mary Pope, <u>Standing in the Light: The Captive Diary of Catharine Carey Logan</u>, Scholastic, 1998.

** Rinaldi, Ann, <u>A Break With Charity</u>, Harcourt Brace, 1992.

Rinaldi, Ann, <u>My Name is America: The Journal of Jasper Jonathan Pierce, A Pilgrim Boy</u>, Scholastic, 2000.

Stainer, M.L., <u>The Lyon's Roar</u>, Chicken Soup Press, 1997.

Stainer, M.L., <u>The Lyon's Cub</u>, Chicken Soup Press, 1998.

Stainer, M.L., <u>The Lyon's Pride</u>, Chicken Soup Press, 1998.

Smith, Patricia Clark, <u>Weetamoo: Heart of the Pocassets, Massachusetts - Rhode Island 1653</u>, Scholastic Press, 2003.

* Less challenging
** More challenging
(in terms of reading level)

AMERICA'S COLONIES OBJECTIVES

Define and be able to use the following terms:

- exploration
- goods
- colony
- ancestors
- marsh
- ceremony
- representative
- disease
- fortress
- missionary
- governor
- comparison
- contrast
- pastor
- ritual
- oath
- economic / economy
- market
- foe
- resource
- persecute
- journal
- founder
- compact
- class
- service
- region
- climate
- port
- piedmont
- industry
- profession
- pewter
- indentured servant
- contract
- passage
- apprentice
- trade
- diagram
- inference
- mercantilism
- tax
- retreat
- allies
- Parliament

Fully answer the following questions:

1. Describe the dangers faced by the American colonies.
2. Explain the reasons why people came to the colonies.
3. Explain how the colonists and Native Americans got along and/or didn't.
4. Explain why leadership and law were important in the colonies.
5. Describe the three regions in Colonial America.
6. Compare and contrast indentured servitude and slavery.
7. Explain the effects mercantilism had on the American colonies.
8. Explain why the French and Indian War was fought and its effects.
9. Explain why tension between the colonists and the king grew.

AMERICA'S COLONIES OBJECTIVES · SUGGESTIONS FOR ANSWERS

Define and be able to use the following terms:

Definitions for terms are provided in the lesson in which they are introduced.

Fully answer the following questions:

1. The early colonists faced conflicts with Natives, harsh weather, difficult farming conditions, low food supplies, unknown lands, and other dangers. These dangers led to the disappearance of Roanoke. Other colonies such as Jamestown and St. Augustine were able to overcome these problems to survive and prosper.

2. Some people like the Puritans and Quakers came to escape persecution by the Church of England. They wanted their own communities where they could worship freely. Others came for economic opportunities, adventure, or to simply build a better life than was available in Europe.

3. Relations between Native Americans and colonists varied. In some cases the two groups got along well - trading and helping one another. In other cases there was violence, stemming largely from colonists taking natives' land without permission or payment.

4. Most colonies were ruled by governors who were either the founders of the colony or appointed by the king. The Mayflower Compact is considered the first written law in the New World. It established a broad outline for government and cooperation among the colonists.

5. The New England Colonies (Massachusetts, Rhode Island, Connecticut, and New Hampshire) were covered in forest and close to water. Despite their long, hard winters, people farmed and established many industries based on ships and trade. The Southern Colonies (Virginia, Maryland, North Carolina, South Carolina, and Georgia) were very different. The region relied heavily on farming with large plantations worked by slaves. The Middle Colonies (New York, Pennsylvania, New Jersey, and Delaware) were much more diverse with qualities of both New England and the South.

6. Both indentured servants and slaves were brought to the colonies to fill the need for labor. Indentured servants were bound to their masters who paid their passage for a fixed period, after which they were freed with supplies and even land in some cases. Slaves were forced from Africa and became the property of their masters forever. Both faced hardships, but indentured servants had hope for their futures.

7. Mercantilism, the belief that power comes from wealth, was the driving force to establish colonies. Mother countries gained materials, labor, and markets for goods, all of which brought great wealth. However, mercantilism also caused tension between colonists and mother countries and among powers themselves.

8. The French and Indian War was fought between England and France over control of the North American colonies. The British won the war, driving the French from the Atlantic coastal colonies. Still, England lost many soldiers and spent huge sums of money, which would bring negative consequences.

9. After the French and Indian War, England was heavily in debt. In addition the king began to think the colonists held too much power in HIS colonies. Therefore, he and his advisors passed many unpopular laws taxing the colonists and exerting more influence over the colonies. These actions eventually lead to the American Revolution.

Land of the Lost

Springboard:
    Students should read "Exploration and Colonies"
and answer the questions.

Objective: The student will be able to explain the dangers faced by colonists arriving in the New World.

Materials:
    Exploration and Colonies (Springboard handout)
The Lost Colony of Roanoke (handout)
On Dangerous Ground (handout)

Terms to know:
    exploration - travel to discover and claim new places
goods - things that can be used, bought, or sold
colony - land settled and ruled by another country
ancestors - family or tribe members in the past

Procedure:
· After reviewing the Springboard, reiterate that *the Age of Exploration led to colonies being established in the New World*. Then explain that *in this lesson the student(s) will learn about England's first attempt to colonize North America.*
· Distribute "The Lost Colony of Roanoke" and "On Dangerous Ground." Have the student(s) study the timeline and map and use the information to complete the analysis form.
· Have the student(s) share and compare answers. (*Answers will vary somewhat, but conflicts with Native Americans, harsh weather, poor food supplies, and unknown and isolated lands were all be dangers faced by early colonists.*)
· Have the student(s) share their theories as to what happened to the Roanoke settlers. (*Theories will of course vary but should be based on lesson information.*) Explain that *to this day, no one knows for certain what really did happen to Roanoke and its settlers*.

Exploration and Colonies

By the late 1400's, people in Europe wanted to trade more with people in Asia. They wanted silk and tea from China, spices from India, and other goods. Europeans also wanted to grow and gain more power by spreading their ways to other lands. So people began to look for new ways to get to the East.

The Age of Exploration, as it came to be known, was started by Prince Henry, the Navigator of Portugal. He trained and paid for explorers to sail the seas. He and others hoped to find faster, cheaper ways to India and China.

In 1492, Christopher Columbus sailed west across the Atlantic Ocean to reach Asia. Instead, his sea voyage brought him to North America. When he went back to Europe, he brought with him many new and exciting goods. Of course, after Columbus, others wanted to take the trip, too. For the next 100 years or so, many explorers sailed to North and South America to claim land for their rulers. Later, more and more people came to settle in this **New World**.

Prince Henry, the Navigator, would **BEST** be described as a/an
    A. teacher.   B. sailor.   C. ruler.   D. explorer.

Which of these statements is a **SUMMARY** of the whole reading?
    A. Europeans wanted to spread their ways around the world.
    B. Christopher Columbus sailed west in order to reach Asia.
    C. The Age of Exploration led to land claims and colonies.
    D. China had better trading goods that Europeans did.

The "New World" in the reading refers to
    A. China.   C. Europe.
    B. Asia.   D. North America.

All of these changes came about because of exploration, **EXCEPT**
    A. new goods.   C. more trade.
    B. new languages.   D. more colonies.

Explain one reason people **WOULD** and one reason **WOULD NOT** want to go the New World in the 1400's and 1500's. _____

_____

_____

_____

_____

By the late 1400's, people in Europe wanted to trade more with people in Asia. They wanted silk and tea from China, spices from India, and other goods. Europeans also wanted to grow and gain more power by spreading their ways to other lands. So people began to look for new ways to get to the East.

The Age of Exploration, as it came to be known, was started by Prince Henry, the Navigator of Portugal. He trained and paid for explorers to sail the seas. He and others hoped to find faster, cheaper ways to India and China.

In 1492, Christopher Columbus sailed west across the Atlantic Ocean to reach Asia. Instead, his sea voyage brought him to North America. When he went back to Europe, he brought with him many new and exciting goods. Of course, after Columbus, others wanted to take the trip, too. For the next 100 years or so, many explorers sailed to North and South America to claim land for their rulers. Later, more and more people came to settle in this **New World**.

Prince Henry, the Navigator would **BEST** be described as a/an
    A. teacher. *   B. sailor.   C. ruler.   D. explorer.
(It says "he was the first to train" others. According to the reading, he did not sail or explore himself; nor was he the ruler but the ruler's son, a prince.)

Which of these statements is a **SUMMARY** of the whole reading?
    A. Europeans wanted to spread their ways around the world.
    B. Christopher Columbus sailed west in order to reach Asia.
    C. The Age of Exploration led to land claims and colonies. *
    D. China had better trading goods that Europeans did.
(Choices A and B are details, and Choice D is an opinion. Choice C includes the most passage information.)

The "New World" in the reading refers to
    A. China.   C. Europe.
    B. Asia.   D. North America. *
(There was nothing "new" about China and Asia as Europeans had already been trading with people there. Until Columbus' journeys, North America was "unknown," at least to Europeans, Africans, and Asians.)

All of these changes came about because of exploration, **EXCEPT**
    A. new goods.   C. more trade.
    B. new languages. *   D. more colonies.
(Exploration was undertaken for more trade and new goods, and colonies were a result. There was no mention of new languages, nor any cause to think they were developed.)

Explain one reason people **WOULD** and one reason **WOULD NOT** want to go the New World in the 1400's and 1500's. *Answers will vary. Reasons in favor could include adventure, more exciting goods, new opportunities, wealth, land, new, unknown possibilities and opportunities, etc. Reasons against could include danger, fear of the unknown, leaving behind family members, "savage natives," etc.*

The Lost Colony of Roanoke

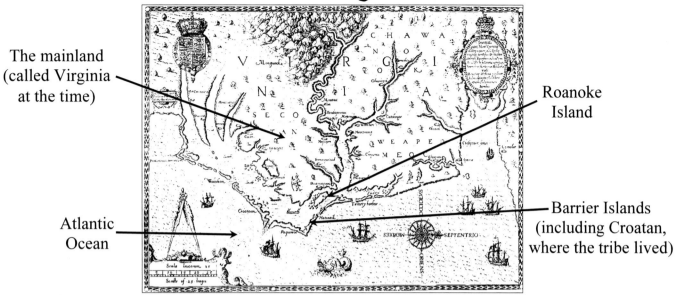

The mainland (called Virginia at the time)

Roanoke Island

Atlantic Ocean

Barrier Islands (including Croatan, where the tribe lived)

1584 — Queen Elizabeth I of England grants Walter Raleigh the right to form a colony in the New World. Raleigh sends a group of men to find a good spot to settle. They return to England with Chief Manteo of the Croatan tribe. All report to Raleigh and the Queen of Roanoke Island.

1585 — The first group of 100 men (many former soldiers) leaves England for Roanoke. Their plan is to build a fort to protect them. They arrive too late to plant crops, and they have a problem. Their leader, Captain Ralph Lane, kills the chief of a local tribe over a stolen silver cup.

1586 — A supply ship arrives and finds the fort empty. The ship's captain leaves 15 men with 2-years-worth of supplies to hold the island. Then he returns to England to tell Raleigh what they found.

1587 — A second group of men, women, and children leave England to settle at Roanoke. This group is led by Governor John White. When they arrive, the 15 men left there are gone. Then their guide quits and leaves them. Chief Manteo, who came back with them, tries to ease tensions with local tribes. The natives refuse to meet the new colonists. Later that year White left for England to get supplies.

1590 — For 3 years White tries to find a way back. But there are no ships since all are in use for England's war with Spain. When White returns to Roanoke, he finds everyone gone. The only clue they left is the word "Croatan" carved into a tree.

1709 — English explorer John Lawson spends time with natives around Roanoke Island. He writes that they claim to have white ancestors. He thinks it must be true since many of them have gray eyes. All other natives he's seen have dark eyes.

On Dangerous Ground

List the dangers or problems you think the Roanoke colonists faced, based on what you can learn from...

THE MAP	THE TIMELINE

What do YOU think may have happened to the settlers at Roanoke? Why? _____

_____

_____

_____

_____

_____

_____

_____

_____

_____

_____

_____

_____

If at First You Don't Succeed...

Objective: Students will compare and contrast colonies at Jamestown and St. Augustine.

Materials:
Pocahontas (Springboard handout)
Captain John Smith (handout)
Pedro Menendez de Aviles (handout)
Compare the Colonies (handout)

Terms to know:
marsh - area of soft, wet, low-lying land
ceremony - a set of acts or movements done in respect or as prayer
representative - someone who speaks and acts on behalf of others
disease - sickness
fortress - walled and guarded place or town
missionary - someone sent to spread religion
governor - the leader of a colony (or state)

Procedure:
· After reviewing the Springboard, explain that *in this lesson the student(s) will learn more about Jamestown and another, even earlier colony, St. Augustine*.
· Distribute "Captain John Smith" and "Pedro Menendez de Aviles." Have the student(s) read the narratives or read them together, underlining or highlighting important passages.
· Then hand out "Compare the Colonies." Have the student(s) work on their own or in groups to complete the organizer.
· Then have them share and compare their answers, using the Teacher page to help guide discussion.
· Have the student(s) share and discuss hardships and challenges faced by characters in the books they're reading. Have them compare and contrast the experiences in the books to those examined in the lesson.

POCAHONTAS

Motoaka, the daughter of a great Powhatan chief, was born around 1595. She lived in the marshes on the coast of Virginia. She was called by the name Pocahontas, which meant "playful and stubborn child." She was still a girl when English setters arrived in Jamestown in 1607. It was most likely the first time she had seen white men.

She is perhaps most famous for saving the life of John Smith, one of the settlers. As the story goes, he had been captured by natives. When he was brought to the chief he was grabbed and stretched over two large stones. Angry men stood all around Smith, ready to beat him to death with clubs. But Pocahontas threw herself on him to save his life. After that her father, the chief, made friends with the white men. And he treated Smith as a son.

There are some who say these things never happened. Others claim these events were just part of a ceremony and Smith was never in any danger. Despite the facts of how they met, Pocahontas became a good friend to the Jamestown colonists.

She brought food when they were hungry. She traded with them for needed items. And time and again she served as a representative of her people. Even when times were tense between the colonists and the Powhatans, she managed to work out deals between them.

After her friend John Smith returned to England, she was taken to live with Jamestown settlers. It was then that she met and married a tobacco farmer named John Rolfe. Their marriage helped bring peace between the colonists and natives at last.

Two years after she married Rolfe, Pocahontas was sent to London. She was to speak to people in England to try to get them to come to Jamestown. While in England she met King James I and many other important people. After seven months, she, Rolfe, and their son set sail for home. Soon after they left, though, Pocahontas became very ill. The ship returned to England, where she died. Pocahontas was buried just outside of London, far from her home and people.

What adjectives might describe Pocahontas? Try to fill all the blanks with words. And be ready to explain your ideas!

_____   _____   _____

_____   _____   _____

_____   _____   _____

_____   _____   _____

_____   _____   _____

Captain John Smith

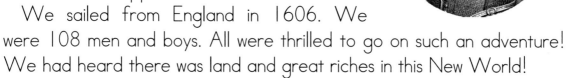

I am Captain John Smith, an explorer from England. I can tell you about the Jamestown colony, as I was there. Our king, James I granted me and my Virginia Company the right to build a colony in the New World. Our goals were to find gold, and a faster route to the Pacific Ocean. We also hoped to learn what happened to Roanoke.

We sailed from England in 1606. We were 108 men and boys. All were thrilled to go on such an adventure! We had heard there was land and great riches in this New World!

But once there, we did not find gold. Instead, we found more insects than we'd ever seen and marsh land! Many among us died from disease. And we could neither find nor grow food. We thought we would starve. I suppose we should have tried harder to get along with the natives. The Powhatan People attacked us often. Once, I took a group of men to find food. Powhatan braves surprised us, killed my men, and took me captive. After a time, though, they let me go in exchange for guns.

The settlers chose me as their leader, and I tried to improve our lives. I was very strict and ordered all to farm. I knew we could not get by trading weapons and supplies with the Natives for food. Then in 1609 I was hurt in an accident. I had to go back to England for treatment of my burns. I hated to leave, but...

The next winter was terrible! In fact, it became known as the "starving time." Most of the settlers died. Those who lived burned chairs, beds, and anything else they could find to keep warm.

Then in 1612 a settler named John Rolfe found something we could grow in Jamestown. Tobacco changed our fortunes! The colonists were able to sell it to buy needed food. They no longer had to depend on the Natives. Their lives further improved when Rolfe married Pocahontas, the daughter of Chief Powhatan. Life was still hard for many more years. Yet the tobacco crops helped Jamestown survive.

Pedro Menendez de Aviles

I am Pedro Menendez de Aviles of Spain. I am pleased to tell you about the place I settled. It is called St. Augustine. In 1565, King Phillip II ordered me to sail to the New World. My task was to help guard Spain's claims and trade routes there. You see, the king learned that the French were also starting colonies nearby. So he told me to build a strong fortress to protect our lands and drive others away.

The king made sure I had all I needed. He sent with me 500 soldiers, 200 sailors, and 100 farmers. He even let some of the men bring their wives and children. When we reached land, we settled on the beach along the Atlantic coast.

Then we held a great feast. We asked the local natives, called the Timucuan People, to come, and they did. After that we got on well with our neighbors. In fact our missionaries spent much time with them to teach of our religion.

Right away, we started to build our forts. As leader, I named myself governor and made all decisions. One such decision was to attack the French settlers at Fort Caroline. We were able to drive them from our land. About this the king was most pleased.

Yet life was still hard. The weather was very hot and wet. There were so many mosquitoes! I think they caused many to be sick. Our land was also hard to farm. Still, we managed. We all thanked the king for keeping us well supplied. For him we worked hard to guard Spain's lands. It is our hope that St. Augustine will be here for a long time. (In fact the Spanish colony guarded Spanish Florida for almost 200 years!)

Compare the Colonies

Jamestown

St. Augustine

How were the two colonies alike?

How were they different?

Which colony do you think fared better? Explain your ideas.

_____

_____

_____

_____

Compare the Colonies
Suggestions for Answers

Jamestown   St. Augustine

How were the two colonies alike?

- Both were settlements in the New World by European countries.
- Life was hard in both colonies.
- Both colonies had problems with insects and diseases.
- Both experienced food shortages.
- Both colonies interacted in some way with Native American peoples.
- Both colonies survived early hardships and problems to become lasting settlements.

How were they different?

- Jamestown was settled by the English in 1606 in Virginia. - The colony was built after the king granted rights to a private company. - Settlers came to get rich. - Only 108 men and boys went at first. - Settlers had poor relations with the Natives. - Settlers elected their leader, John Smith - Settlers had to trade with the Powhatan People for food. - The colony survived because they learned how to grow tobacco.	- St. Augustine was settled by the Spanish in 1565 in Florida. - The colony was built on the orders of the king. - Settlers came to defend Spanish lands in the New World. - 500 soldiers, 200 sailors, and 100 farmers went, along with some families. - Settlers got along well with Natives. - Pedro Menendez de Aviles appointed himself governor of the colony. - Settlers were supported and supplied by the king. - Settlers were successful at protecting Spanish lands for almost 200 years.

Which colony do you think fared better? Explain your ideas.

Answers may vary and should be well-reasoned. Both were successful in their own ways. Jamestown was the first successful English colony in North America, while St. Augustine holds that distinction for Spain.

©InspirEd Educators, Inc.

Free to Be You and Me

Springboard:
 Students should study the "Puritans and Quakers" Venn diagram
 and answer the questions.

Objective: The student will be able to explain why religious groups such as the Puritans and Quakers came to the American colonies.

Materials: Puritans and Quakers (Springboard handout)
 Laws of the (Eng)Land (handout)
 What Could They Do? (handout)

Terms to know: **comparison** - way or ways things are alike
 contrast - way or ways things differ
 pastor - church leader
 ritual - action or ceremony practiced regularly
 oath - serious promise often made publicly

Procedure:

· After reviewing the Springboard, explain that *religious groups like the Puritans and the Quakers came to the colonies in large numbers in the 1600's, often to escape the Church of England, the only legal church in the country*. Go on to explain that *this lesson examines why*.

· Distribute "Laws of the (Eng)Land" and explain that *these were laws that were passed in England in regards to groups such as the Puritans and Quakers*. Review the laws together and have the student(s) respond to each law in the space provided in order to check for understanding.

· Then hand out "What Could They Do?" Have the student(s) work individually, in pairs or small groups to complete the problem-solving form.

· Have the student(s) or groups share and compare their ideas. *(Answers will vary. Some students may argue they could have gone to other places in Europe or give up their religious beliefs and swear loyalty to the king. However starting their own communities in the New World would have been a better option for these people. They could practice their religions freely, and putting distance between themselves and the king would allow them to feel safer. They could also establish their own colonies based on their beliefs, as opposed to trying to "fit in" somewhere else, etc.)*

· Close the lesson by explaining that *many of these groups, who were persecuted in their homeland, eventually made their way to the American colonies*.

Puritans and Quakers

Puritans
- Wanted to "purify" the Church of England, not separate completely
- Lived simply and valued hard work
- Dressed plainly and had very strict rules to live by
- Included the Pilgrims who of Plymouth, Massachusetts (1620)
- All beliefs and practices came from the Bible
- Education of children important; had to read and understand Bible
- Had baptisms and some other religious ceremonies
- Pastors very important ; main job to preach about the Bible

Both
- Did not agree with Church of England
- Were treated badly by Church of England
- Wanted their freedom to practice religion
- Wanted own communities
- Left England for American colonies

Quakers
- Completely separated from Church of England
- Also called the "Religious Society of Friends"
- Did not practice any ceremonies
- Tried to live lives as good examples for others
- Believe God talks to people; a "light from within"
- Believe all people are equal
- Against slavery and war
- Some pastors, but not important
- First came to America in 1656 to Pennsylvania colony
- Did not view education as important
- View Bible as one of many books to be read

The graphic shown is called a
    A. pie chart.   B. bar graph.   C. Venn diagram.   D. map key.

Both the Puritans and Quakers could be described in all these ways, **EXCEPT** as
    A. religious groups.   C. colonists.
    B. from England.   D. pastors.

One **COMPARISON** (way they're alike) between the two groups is:
    A. Quakers did not consider the Bible as important as the Puritans did.
    B. Puritans were much stricter about behavior and dress than the Quakers.
    C. Both groups left England to set up colonies and live in the New World.
    D. Only the Puritans practiced certain religious ceremonies such as baptism.

One **CONTRAST** (way they're different) between the two groups is:
    A. Education was not as important to the Quakers as it was to the Puritans.
    B. Neither Puritans nor Quakers were members of the Church of England.
    C. Puritans and Quakers wanted to practice their religion freely and safely.
    D. Both groups were unhappy with the way they were treated in England.

Puritans and Quakers
Answers and Explanations

Puritans (left circle):
- Wanted to "purify" the Church of England, not separate completely
- Lived simply and valued hard work
- Dressed plainly and had very strict rules to live by
- Included the Pilgrims who of Plymouth, Massachusetts (1620)
- All beliefs and practices came from the Bible
- Education of children important; had to read and understand Bible
- Had baptisms and some other religious ceremonies
- Pastors very important ; main job to preach about the Bible

Both (center):
- Did not agree with Church of England
- Were treated badly by Church of England
- Wanted their freedom to practice religion
- Wanted own communities
- Left England for American colonies

Quakers (right circle):
- Completely separated from Church of England
- Also called the "Religious Society of Friends"
- Did not practice any ceremonies
- Tried to live lives as good examples for others
- Believe God talks to people; a "light from within"
- Believe all people are equal
- Against slavery and war
- Some pastors, but not important
- First came to America in 1656 to Pennsylvania colony
- Did not view education as important
- View Bible as one of many books to be read

The graphic shown is called a

    A. pie chart.   B. bar graph.   C. Venn diagram. *   D. map key.
    (Even if students don't recognize a Venn, they should know it is not a map. The words "pie" and "bar" should also offer clues to eliminate Choices A and B.)

Both the Puritans and Quakers could be described in all these ways, **EXCEPT** as

    A. religious groups   B. from England   C. colonists   D. pastors *
    (The information identifies pastors as MEMBERS of each group. Students should be able to determine the other choices are true by the Venn information.)

One **COMPARISON** (way they're alike) between the two groups is:

    A. Quakers did not consider the Bible as important as the Puritans did.
    B. Puritans were much stricter about behavior and dress than the Quakers.
    C. Both groups left England to set up colonies and live in the New World. *
    D. Only the Puritans practiced certain religious ceremonies such as baptism.
    (Choice B is the only one that explains how the two groups are the SAME.)

One **CONTRAST** (way they're different) between the two groups is:

    A. Education was not as important to the Quakers as it was to the Puritans. *
    B. Neither Puritans nor Quakers were members of the Church of England.
    C. Puritans and Quakers wanted to practice their religion freely and safely.
    D. Both groups were unhappy with the way they were treated in England.
    (Choice A is the only one that explains how the two groups are DIFFERENT.)

Laws of the (Eng)Land

DIRECTIONS: Read each law passed by the British government. Explain how each might affect your life if you were a member of a group like the Puritans or the Quakers:

The Act of Uniformity (1622): This law required Church of England prayers be said and rituals done at all church services.

_____

_____

_____

The Quaker Act (1622): This law made it a crime to not swear an oath to be loyal to the king. (Quakers do not believe in taking oaths or swearing to anything.)

_____

_____

_____

The Conventicle Act (1664): This law makes it a crime to hold any religious meetings other than those approved by the Church of England.

_____

_____

_____

The Five Mile Act (1662): This law made it a crime for people who leave the Church of England to live within five miles of a church or the town around it.

_____

_____

_____

_____

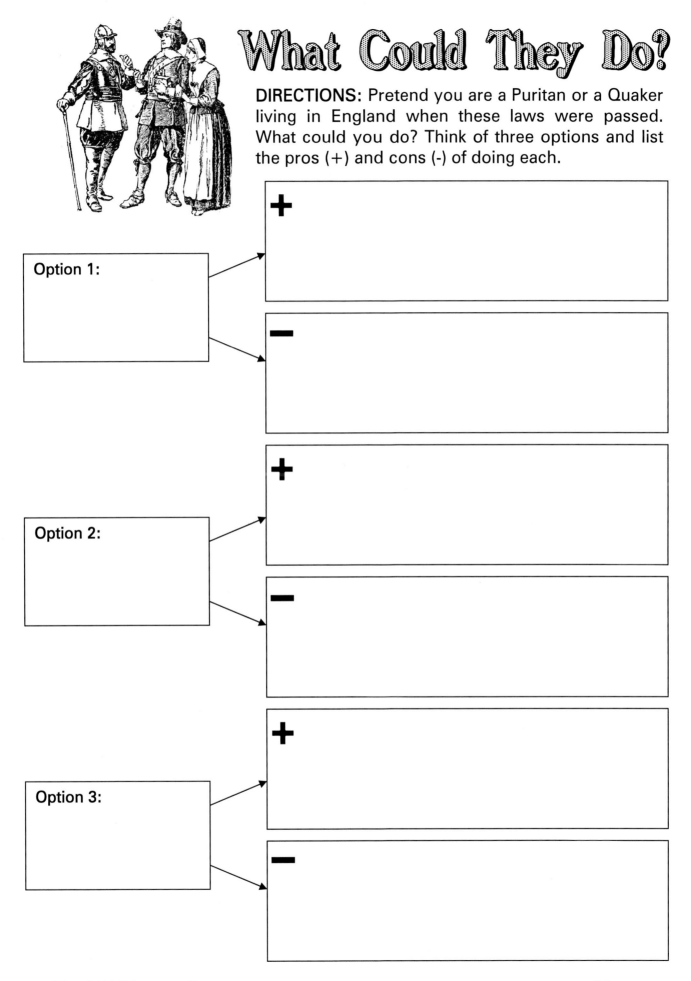

What Could They Do?

DIRECTIONS: Pretend you are a Puritan or a Quaker living in England when these laws were passed. What could you do? Think of three options and list the pros (+) and cons (-) of doing each.

Option 1:

+

−

Option 2:

+

−

Option 3:

+

−

Sign Me Up!

Springboard:
Students should complete the "What Were They Thinking?" handout.

Objective: The student will be able to describe various reasons why people left England to come to the colonies.

Materials:
What Were They Thinking? (Springboard handout)
Come Sail Away... (handout)
To Guide Your Way (handout)

Terms to know:
economic / economy - having to do with money and business
market - *(v)* to sell; *(n)* buyers being sold to

Procedure:

- After reviewing the Springboard, explain that *in this lesson the student(s) will pretend to work for a company to attract people to go to the colonies.*
- Distribute "Come Sail Away..." and "To Guide Your Way." Review the chart information and assignment requirements, and have the student(s) choose (or assign) a colony from the chart. They should work independently, in pairs, or small groups to research using the note taking form and create the poster or flyer.
- **NOTE:** This assignment can be as in depth as desired and could span two class periods depending on the amount of research you want the student(s) to do. To shorten the assignment, have the student(s) skip the research and use their own ideas and the chart information to complete their advertisement.
- Have them share and evaluate their work. Lead a follow-up discussion, using the following questions as a guide: (*Answers will vary*)
  - **?** Why did the character(s) in the book you're reading come to the colonies?
  - **?** Did things work out for him / her according to their plans? Why or why not?
  - **?** Do you think that most colonists "found what they were looking for" in the New World? Why or why not?
  - **?** If you lived at that time, what might have motivated you to make a long ocean-crossing to go to the Americas?

What Were They Thinking?

DIRECTIONS: Read each statement below and…
1. Write if you think the person came to the colonies for economic reasons (E), religious reasons (R), or other reasons (O).
2. Underline the words and phrases that offered clues for your answers.
3. If you decide on "other reasons," write what you think the reason was after the statement.

_____ "I have made a lot of money in business in England. If I opened more stores in the New World, I could make even more."

_____ "I cannot find a job here! Maybe in the New World I could get work and be able to feed my family."

_____ "I am so afraid that we will be put in jail for holding these meetings."

_____ "Life here is boring. I should get on a ship and go to the New World. I'm sure life there would be more interesting."

_____ "My brothers and sisters, we need to be an example for the world to see! We must show others how to truly serve God."

_____ "I am proud to be English. Mine is the strongest country on earth! We will spread our greatness around the world!"

_____ "Since my father has so many sons, there is no land left for me. If I go to the New World, I can own as much land as I want!"

_____ "The King has too much power. He controls our lives. We need to get as far away from him as possible!"

_____ "I am an officer in England's army, but there are no wars to fight. There is nothing to do!"

Write a "quote" someone coming to the colonies might have said:_____

_____

_____

_____

What Were They Thinking? ~ Suggested Answers

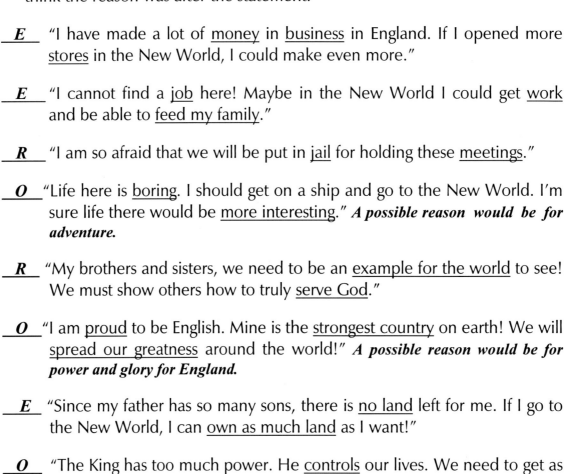

DIRECTIONS: Read each statement below and…
1. Write if you think the person came to the colonies for economic reasons (E), religious reasons (R), or other reasons (O).
2. Underline words and phrases that provided clues for your answers.
3. If you decide on "other reasons," write what you think the reason was after the statement.

_E_ "I have made a lot of <u>money</u> in <u>business</u> in England. If I opened more <u>stores</u> in the New World, I could make even more."

_E_ "I cannot find a <u>job</u> here! Maybe in the New World I could get <u>work</u> and be able to <u>feed my family</u>."

_R_ "I am so afraid that we will be put in <u>jail</u> for holding these <u>meetings</u>."

_O_ "Life here is <u>boring</u>. I should get on a ship and go to the New World. I'm sure life there would be <u>more interesting</u>." ***A possible reason would be for adventure.***

_R_ "My brothers and sisters, we need to be an <u>example for the world</u> to see! We must show others how to truly <u>serve God</u>."

_O_ "I am <u>proud</u> to be English. Mine is the <u>strongest country</u> on earth! We will <u>spread our greatness</u> around the world!" ***A possible reason would be for power and glory for England.***

_E_ "Since my father has so many sons, there is <u>no land</u> left for me. If I go to the New World, I can <u>own as much land</u> as I want!"

_O_ "The King has too much power. He <u>controls</u> our lives. We need to get as <u>far away from him</u> as possible!" ***A possible reason would be more freedom.***

_O_ "I am an <u>officer</u> in England's <u>army</u>, but there are <u>no wars</u> to fight. There is <u>nothing to do</u>!" ***A possible reason could be to protect England's lands in the New World or, again, adventure.***

Write another statement that someone coming to the colonies might say: ***Answers will vary but should reflect what students have learned about why people came to the colonies.***

©InspirEd Educators, Inc.

Come Sail Away...

The Mission:

For this assignment you work for a shipping company. Your job is to get as many people as you can to buy tickets to the New World on your company's ships.

The Requirements:

- Study the chart below and choose one colony to market. You should use the note-taking form to guide research on your colony. Then create a poster or flyer to convince someone to buy a ticket and sail to the colony you picked.
- Keep in mind the people that you want to attract when making your ad. Include points that would appeal to your target market!
- Make sure you include all the important information from your notes in your ad.
- Keep in mind the points scored on in the "Market Analysis" (below) as you work.

Colony	From	Purpose
St. Augustine	Spain	Protection (against the French) and power
Jamestown	England	Trade and riches
Plymouth	England	Religious freedom
New York	Holland	Trade and riches
Massachusetts Bay	England	Religious freedom
New Hampshire	England	Trade and riches
Maryland	England	Riches and religious freedom
Delaware	Sweden	Trade and riches
North Carolina	England	Trade and riches
New Jersey	England	Trade and riches
South Carolina	England	Trade and riches
Pennsylvania	England	Religious freedom
Louisiana	France	Control of the Mississippi River for trade
Georgia	England	Protection (against Spanish)

Market Analy$is

Rate your work using this scale:

4 - Excellent   3 - Good   2 - Fair   1 - Poor   0 - Unacceptable

	Student	Teacher
Includes all it should	_____	_____
Made people WANT to go	_____	_____
Geared to target group	_____	_____
Neat and creative	_____	_____

GRADE:

TO GUIDE YOUR WAY

DIRECTIONS: Use the questions to guide your research on the colony you choose.

COLONY:_____ **PURPOSE:**_____

What kind of people came to, or would want to come to your colony? What are some things that might appeal to them? (pictures, phrases, etc.)

What does your colony offer that would appeal to people?

What is the colony like? (weather, physical features, etc.) How would it's features etc. appeal to your target market?

What, if anything, is required of people in the colony?

Anything else that would help convince someone to buy a ticket?

Friend or Foe?

Objective: The student will be able to explain some of the interactions between Native Americans and colonists.

Materials: Your Worst Nightmare (Springboard handout)
        Fast Friends / Fierce Foes (2-page handout)

Terms to know: **foe** - enemy

Procedure:

· After discussion of the Springboard, explain that *though many colonists feared the Native Americans, relationships between the two groups widely varied, depending on the circumstances*. Go on to explain that *this lesson examines those relationships*.

· Distribute the "Fast Friends / Fierce Foes" pages and review the directions. Then have the student(s) work individually, in pairs, or small groups to complete the handouts.

· Have them share their ideas and explanations. *(Answers may vary but should be explained.)* Discuss the following questions while reviewing each numbered scenario *(Answers may vary.):*

1. How do you think interactions with the white settlers helped or hurt the Native people?

2. Again, what positive and negative effects did the natives' helping have on their tribe?

3. Does this information change your views about the first two situations?

4. What POSSIBLE reason could the Natives have had to kill the settlers? *(The settlers probably moved into the tribe's lands. Most likely no payment was made, nor is it likely that the settlers had Natives' permission to take the land.)*
Do you think the murders could be excused for these reasons?
How do you think other settlers reacted to the murders?

5. Do you think the settlers helped or hurt the Native children?
Do you think the settlers were right in trying to teach their religion? Why?

6. How do you think trading with the French helped or hurt Native Americans?

7. Do you think the Native people were as happy to get pots, pans, knives, cloth, etc. as the French were to get furs? Why?

Your Worst Nightmare?

DIRECTIONS: Pretend you are in Europe in the 1600's. You are poor and think the American colonies may offer a chance for a better life. But you also know there are dangers. What do YOU fear? Explain what you think of each "danger" and why.

Bears, wolves, snakes, etc. - _____

_____

_____

_____

_____

Not enough food - _____

_____

_____

_____

_____

Bad weather - _____

_____

_____

_____

_____

Native attacks - _____

_____

_____

_____

_____

Other? - _____

_____

_____

_____

_____

FAST FRIENDS \ FIERCE FOES

DIRECTIONS: Read about each way the natives and colonists "got along." Mark an X on the line for each to show what you think. Then explain your ideas in the space below.

1. The native people were quite friendly. The colonists met the chief of a local tribe. He helped them choose a good spot for their village. Then he and others showed the colonists plants they could eat and gave them seeds to plant. They even taught the colonists how to cook all the new foods!

FAST   **FIERCE**

FRIENDS   **FOES**

2 The people in the colony were hungry. It was as likely as not that they would have all starved to death. Winter was long that year and started early. The little stores of food they had were not enough to survive, and they knew it. Then the local native people brought them food! They were so thankful to be alive!

FAST   **FIERCE**

FRIENDS   **FOES**

3. Many of the local natives were kind to the settlers. And the settlers were kind in turn. Their children even played together. But soon many native children fell ill. They had red spots all over them and felt hot. Then they died. Many parents also died. Most in the tribe, in fact, died of the pox in that first year.

FAST   **FIERCE**

FRIENDS   **FOES**

4. The family moved from the coast inland. They were so happy to have more land! They could farm and keep more animals! They cut down trees to make room for crops. And they were using the logs to build their new home. Then, one night a group of natives came and killed the whole family.

FAST   **FIERCE**

←————————————————————————————————————→

FRIENDS   **FOES**

5. The people of the town liked the natives. But they also worried about them. The "poor savages" had no church, and religion was VERY important to their colony! The people decided to send missionaries to work with the native children. The missionaries could teach them about God. And they could learn English at the same time. Perhaps then they would one day live as they should.

FAST   **FIERCE**

←————————————————————————————————————→

FRIENDS   **FOES**

6. The French came to Quebec to trade furs. The native people knew the land and how to find the animals there. They knew how to trap them and to clean their pelts. Beaver, otter, and other animals' furs are prized in Europe. The French traded items the native people could use for the furs. They brought metal knives, pots, tools, glass beads, wool cloth, and other goods to "buy" the furs, which brought high prices.

FAST   **FIERCE**

←————————————————————————————————————→

FRIENDS   **FOES**

Follow the Leader

Objective: The student will be able to explain the contributions of various colonial leaders.

Materials:
The London Company (Springboard handout)
Colonial Leader Cards (card cut-outs)
Colonial Leaders (handout)
Comparing Notes (handout)

Terms to know:
resource - something in nature that is useful valuable
persecute - cruel treatment of a person or group
journal - daily log or diary
founder - one who starts or sets up something

Procedure:

· After reviewing the Springboard, explain that _there were several individuals as well as companies that established some of the American colonies_. Go on to explain that _in this lesson the student(s) will learn about some famous colonial leaders_.

· **For group instruction** divide the class into six groups, giving each a "Colonial Leader Card." Instruct the groups to create a short skit to tell the story of the person on their card. (**NOTE**: Depending on ability level, you could have the students conduct their own research instead of using the biography cards. In that case simply assign a leader to each group.)

· **For individualized instruction** have the student either research or review the "Colonial Leader Cards" to complete the "Colonial Leaders" handout.

· Have the groups present their skits as others take notes on the "Colonial Leaders" handout, and review the handout.

· Then distribute the "Comparing Notes" Venn diagram. The student(s) can work individually, in pairs, or in combined groups to compare and contrast two leaders.

The London Company

The London Company was started in 1606 in England. It and the Plymouth Company were both part of the Virginia Company. The king at the time, James I, granted the right to colonize lands. The London Company was given land along the Atlantic coast stretching from what is now North Carolina to Connecticut. In areas where land overlapped with the Plymouth Company, settlements had to be at least 100 miles apart to avoid any **conflicts**.

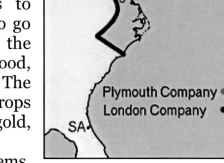

The London Company sent colonists to Jamestown in 1607. They asked people to go and work for seven years. In exchange, the London Company paid for their travel, food, and land. It also agreed to protect them. The company would make money from the crops the settlers grew and other resources (gold, they hoped) from the colony.

Sadly, Jamestown had many problems. Many settlers got sick and died. Those who lived spent all their time and energy just trying to survive! They did not find gold and could not grow crops. By 1612 the London Company had lost money. And it had trouble getting more people to go to America. People had heard stories and didn't want to take the risk. Things were so bad by 1624, the king took over the company. Virginia then became a royal colony.

The word "conflicts" **MOST NEARLY** means
    A. lands.   B. troubles.   C. farms.   D. bridges.

Which word describes how **MOST** English viewed the trip to America in the early 1600's?
    A. royal.   B. inviting.   C. risky.   D. settling.

Which sentence states the main idea of the reading?
    A. The London Company was one part of the Virginia Company.
    B. Gold in the New World made the London Company a success.
    C. London Company was the first owner of the Virginia colony.
    D. Many problems caused Virginia to be named a royal colony.

What kind of "stories" do you think reached England that kept people from going to the New World? _____

_____

_____

_____

The London Company was started in 1606 in England. It and the Plymouth Company were both part of the Virginia Company. The king at the time, James I, granted the right to colonize lands. The London Company was given land along the Atlantic coast stretching from what is now North Carolina to Connecticut. In areas where land overlapped with the Plymouth Company, settlements had to be at least 100 miles apart to avoid any **conflicts**.

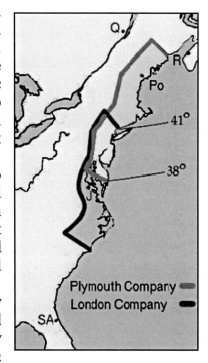

Plymouth Company
London Company

The London Company sent colonists to Jamestown in 1607. They asked people to go and work for seven years. In exchange, the London Company paid for their travel, food, and land. It also agreed to protect them. The company would make money from the crops the settlers grew and other resources (gold, they hoped) from the colony.

Sadly, Jamestown had many problems. Many settlers got sick and died. Those who lived spent all their time and energy just trying to survive! They did not find gold and could not grow crops. By 1612 the London Company had lost money. And it had trouble getting more people to go to America. People had heard stories and didn't want to take the risk. Things were so bad by 1624, the king took over the company. Virginia then became a royal colony.

The word "conflicts" **MOST NEARLY** means
      A. lands.   B. troubles. *   C. farms.   D. bridges.
      (If students don't know the meaning of the word "conflicts," they should substitute each choice into the sentence and see which makes sense. Choice B is the only one that does.)

Which word describes how **MOST** English viewed the trip to America in the early 1600's?
      A. royal.   B. inviting.   C. risky. *   D. settling.
      (Few people wanted to take the London Company's offer, seeing it as too risky.)

Which sentence states the main idea of the reading?
      A. The London Company was one part of the Virginia Company.
      B. Gold in the New World made the London Company a success.
      C. London Company was the first owner of the Virginia colony.
      D. Many problems caused Virginia to be named a royal colony. *
      (Choices A and C are details, and Choice B is false. Though not a "perfect" summary statement, Choice D provides the most information from the reading.)

What kind of "stories" do you think reached England that kept people from going to the New World? *Answers may vary and may include: the "starving time," difficulties with natives, and other hardships from Jamestown that would frighten people and discourage them from going to the colonies.*

Colonial Leader Cards

William Bradford (Plymouth Colony, Massachusetts)

At age 17 William Bradford became a member of a church that wanted to leave the Church of England. When the king began to persecute them, he and others ran away to Holland. He and other church leaders loved England and wanted to be "English." Yet they all agreed it would be safer for them to leave and move far from the king so they could live in peace.

Bradford and others sailed to America on the *Mayflower* in 1620. The first year was very hard. Half the settlers died. But the colony survived, and Bradford became its first governor. He was strict but fair. In fact, when the *Mayflower* returned to England in 1621, no one chose to leave. Bradford led the colony for 36 years. Thanks to his journals, we now know a great deal about Plymouth. The journals, published years later, were called Of Plymouth Plantation.

John Winthrop (Massachusetts Bay)

When John Winthrop was young, he got very sick and almost died. His illness led him to become a Puritan and speak out against the Church of England. As an adult he, like others who left the Church of England, was persecuted for his beliefs.

He asked King Charles and was granted the right to start the Massachusetts Bay Colony in 1630. Then he and 700 others left England for the New World on the *Arbella*. While on their journey, he told his group that they would be "a city upon a hill." He meant that they should show others how to live a good and proper life.

When Winthrop's group arrived in Massachusetts, the colonists chose him as their leader 12 times! Still, his actions did not always please the settlers. He had many conflicts with church leaders. He banished Anne Hutchinson who preached against Puritan beliefs. He also forced Roger Williams out of the colony for speaking out about the way the natives were treated. Winthrop's journals were published as The History of New England. His work provides much of what we know today about the history of Massachusetts.

Roger Williams (Rhode Island)

Roger Williams grew up in England. He lived in a town not far from where many Puritans were persecuted. Williams believed strongly in religious freedom. After he went to college he became a preacher. His ideas about religion got him into trouble, so he chose to leave England for the New World.

He sailed in 1631 on the *Lyon* and arrived in the Massachusetts Bay colony. His ideas about the native people again brought him trouble. He fought with John Winthrop, the colony's leader. Williams argued that settlers should pay for the land they took from the natives. Winthrop told him to leave the colony and go back to England. But Williams ran away before he could be sent back.

Instead of leaving, he bought land from the natives near the shore and named his settlement Providence. He was granted rights to the new colony in 1663. Providence was a place where people such as Quakers, Jews, and Baptists could live freely. He wrote Key Into the Language of America, the first study of Native American language. His book helped make trade and living with native people easier.

Colonial Leader Cards

John Mason (New Hampshire)

John Mason was a sailor from England who went to the New World. His life there really started in Newfoundland near the east coast of Canada. There, he served as governor in 1615. He also explored the area, made maps, and wrote about the land.

A few years later, Mason and another man were offered land in New England by a company there. The two men split the land, Mason getting the half to the south. There he set up a fishing colony. He named his new colony New Hampshire, after the town he was from in England. Mason sent many settlers to New Hampshire and spent a great deal of money building towns and fortresses. New Hampshire, which had first been part of Massachusetts, became a royal colony 1679.

William Penn (Pennsylvania)

William Penn was born into a family of high rank in England. When he was 15, Penn met a Quaker missionary and learned about the religion. Later, he began going to Quaker meetings. This greatly angered his family, and they sent him away.

It was then he went to live with Quakers. He traveled with George Fox, the religion's founder. With Fox and others, Penn was put in jail many more times before leaving England for the New World. He asked King Charles II to grant him and other Quakers the right to start a colony. The king agreed, and in 1682 Penn sailed on the *Welcome* for America.

He named the new colony Pennsylvania to honor his father. The colony was known for religious freedom and treating the native people well. Penn paid them for land and was well-liked by the natives. He would pay the natives visits with no guards, showing his bravery. He helped his friend George Fox write a journal about the Quaker religion. This was the first writing on that subject.

James Oglethorpe (Georgia)

James Oglethorpe was a British general. He cared deeply about England's poor people. He also wanted to help people who were in jail for owing money. Oglethorpe asked King George II if he could start a colony. He hoped to create a place where poor people could go for a better life. He was granted the right and sailed from England in 1732 on the *Anne*.

Oglethorpe named his colony Georgia after the king. As leader, he was very strict. The settlers had to build forts because the Spanish were just to the south in Florida. And the Spanish did attack! Yet Oglethorpe was a good general and saved the land. This earned him great respect among his settlers. On the other hand he did not allow rum or slaves in his new colony which made some quite mad. The colonists wrote the king about him so much that the king ordered Oglethorpe back to England.

In England, Oglethorpe joined the army again and fought for his country once more. Still there were many who spoke ill of him for his actions in Georgia.

Colonial Leaders

William Bradford -

John Winthrop -

Roger Williams -

John Mason -

William Penn -

James Oglethorpe -

COMPARING NOTES

DIRECTIONS: Use the Venn diagram to compare and contrast two colonial leaders.

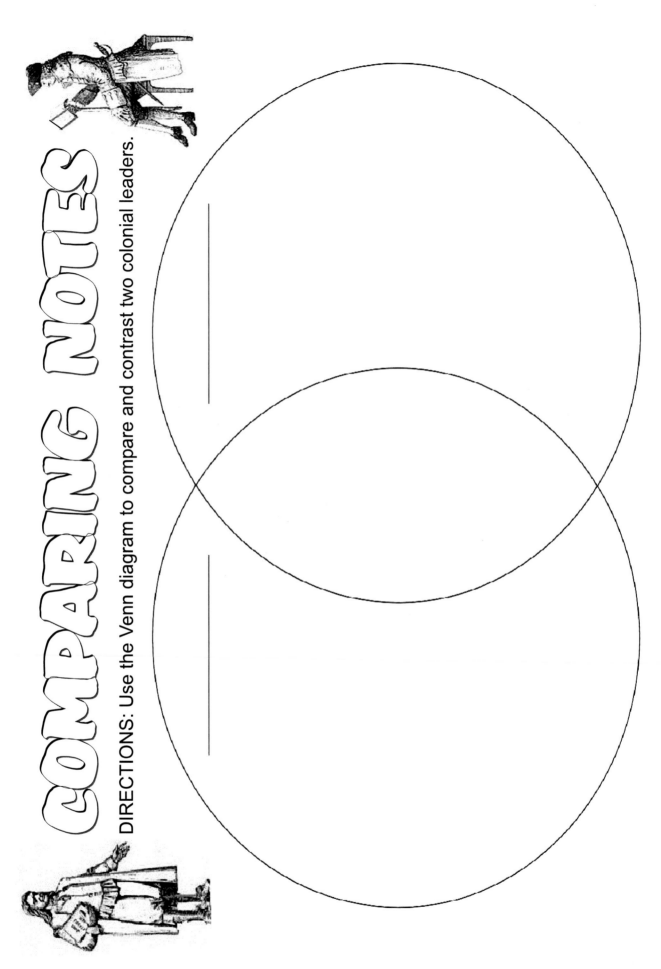

Order!

Springboard:
Students should complete the "What is Law?" handout.
(*Answers will vary but should spark discussion.*)

Objective: The student will be able to explain the importance of law in the colonies.

Materials:

What is Law? (Springboard handout)
Brainstorming Rules (handout or transparency)
Colonial Laws (handout)
The Mayflower Compact (handout or transparency)

Terms to know:

compact - an agreement

Procedure:

·   After discussing the Springboard, remind the student(s) that *the colonies were mostly ruled by governors* (refer to last lesson). *But in addition to leaders, the colonies also needed rules or laws to keep order.* Go on to explain that *this lesson examines the kinds of laws that were needed.*

·   Distribute or display the "Brainstorming Rules" and review them. Then hand out "Colonial Laws" and have the student(s) begin brainstorming in response to the scenario question. (**NOTE:** Ideally, brainstorming is done in pairs or groups, since the interaction encourages the flow of ideas.) **For group instruction** have students work in groups, following the rules of brainstorming and recording their ideas. **For individual instruction** work with your student to generate and record ideas.

·   Have the student(s) share / compare their answers. If sharing, once an idea is read, all with the same idea should check it off their list. In this way, compile a class list.

·   Then display or distribute "The Mayflower Compact." (**NOTE:** This version has simplified language for use with younger students. Accelerated students can read the original language online.)

·   Read the document together and discuss the following questions:
    ? Why do you think the colonists wrote this? (*Answers may vary.*)
    ? How do you think something like this can help the colony succeed? (*It sets guidelines for behavior that will benefit all and increase the chances for survival and success.*)

·   Then revisit the list of rules compiled for a new colony. Have the student(s) compare and contrast their ideas with those in the Mayflower Compact. (*Answers will vary. The student rules and laws are likely more specific, while the Mayflower Compact provided a broad outline for government.*)

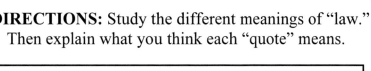

WHAT IS LAW?

DIRECTIONS: Study the different meanings of "law." Then explain what you think each "quote" means.

law *(noun)* - 1. rule that tells how to behave 2. people who make others obey the rules (police, judges, etc.)

1. "above the law" - _____
   _____
   _____

2. "break the law" - _____
   _____
   _____

3. "lay down the law" - _____
   _____
   _____

4. "long arm of the law" - _____
   _____
   _____

5. "wrong side of the law" - _____
   _____
   _____

6. "take the law into your own hands" - _____
   _____
   _____

7. "my word is law" - _____
   _____
   _____

* **WHAT DO YOU THINK?** Do you think laws are important? Explain your reasons._____
_____
_____
_____
_____

Brainstorming Rules!

1. List as many ideas as you can.

2. All group members should offer ideas.

3. Be creative. The more ideas you think of, the better!

4. All ideas are welcome no matter how silly or far out they seem.

5. No judgments should be made about anyone's ideas. (Groaning, frowning, and laughing are some things **NOT** to do.)

6. Build on others' ideas whenever you can.

7. Write down all ideas so the whole group can see them.

8. Set a time limit (such as 20 minutes) for the brainstorming.

9. Talk about the ideas on your list after the brainstorming time is over.

COLONIAL LAWS

PRETEND: You are a member of a group of colonists who have just arrived in the New World. What rules or laws do you think would help you and others survive and succeed?

The Mayflower Compact

In the name of God. We, whose names are listed below are loyal to our King. We have come to the New World to please our God and honor our King and country.

We swear, in the presence of God and each other, that we have planned a government to help us keep order and survive. All laws we write will be fair and equal for all. All laws will be for the good of the colony. And we all promise to obey them.

We sign this promise at Cape Cod on the eleventh of November 1620, during the reign of our ruler, King James of England.

Signed,

John Carver
Edmon Margeson
Francis Eaton
Stephen Hopkins
William Brewster
Richard Clarke
Moses Fletcher
Thomas Rogers
Samuel Fuller
Thomas English
Thomas Williams
Edward Fuller
William White

Richard Warren
William Bradford
Peter Brown
James Chilton
Edward Tilly
Myles Standish
Richard Gardiner
John Goodman
Thomas Tinker
Christopher Martin
Edward Doty
Gilbert Winslow

John Turner
John Howland
Edward Winslow
Richard Britteridge
John Billington
Francis Cooke
John Alden
John Allerton
Degory Priest
John Ridgdale
William Mullins
Edward Leister

Walking in Their Shoes

Objective: The student will be able to describe what everyday life was like in a typical colonial town.

Materials: Colonial Towns (Springboard handout)
Colonial Life (handout)

Terms to know: **class** - rank among others (by money, birth, etc.)
service - work that does not make a product (teacher, doctor, lawyer, etc.)

Procedures:

· After reviewing the Springboard, explain that *in this lesson the student(s) will learn more about life in colonial America.* Go on to explain that *this lesson looks in particular at what life would have been like in a colonial town.*

· Distribute the "Colonial Life" page and explain that *this is a list of information about colonial life.*

· After the student(s) have studied the colonial list, have them write at least three journal entries as a colonist on their own paper using information from list and/or the Springboard. (**NOTE:** Encourage creativity by having students add drawings, "old" paper, or other details to make their journals appear more "real.")

· Have the student(s) share their journals and discuss. *(Journals will vary and should reflect information about what activities were done on the various days of the week. For example if their journal describes a Sunday, it would make sense for the person to go to church.)*

· Have student(s) compare and contrast what they learned in the lesson to life in the books they are reading using a blank Venn diagram, other organizer, or in discussion, as desired.

Colonial Towns

Most people who came to the colonies were farmers. When they arrived they were given land. Those of higher classes were given larger tracts of land. Most of the first colonists were men. Later, men began to bring their families. The farmers worked long hours just to grow enough to eat. Life was hard and most people lived far from one another.

Colonists lived in wooden farmhouses. Houses were small and most were only one level. The fireplace was the center of the home. It was used to cook and keep warm. Most houses only had two rooms. One was for sitting during the day and sleeping at night. The other was where people ate and worked.

As more and more people came to the colonies, people began moving farther from the coast. Towns grew as farmers came to trade their food for needed items. Colonial towns were busy places. As time went on, more and more people opened shops. They sold goods and services to colonists in towns and from the areas around them. By trading with the English, the shops were able to sell goods like tea and cloth. Many people in the colonies wanted goods from England or elsewhere. Trade helped businesses grow and towns became bigger and more important.

DIRECTIONS: List the pros and cons of farm and town life in the boxes.

FARM +:	TOWN +:

FARM -:	TOWN -:

COLONIAL LIFE

- Schools were usually in small one-room houses.

- Boys went to school until they were about 9 or 10.

- Some girls went to "dame schools" in someone's home.

- Most children were taught at home.

- Most of what children learned was about religion.

- People ate vegetables and meats. They drank tea or cider.

- Religion was very important!

- People washed on Saturday nights to be clean for church on Sunday.

- Everyone spent all day Sunday in church.

- No work (other than cooking meals) was done on Sundays. Sunday dishes were washed on Monday.

- Puritans believed in hard work and living simple lives.

- Most things they did were at church or with church friends.

- Colonial families were often very large.

- Most homes were crowded so good manners were important.

- It was not polite to hum, fidget, or kill insects and other pests (such as mice) in front of others.

- Loud talking or laughing was also seen as rude.

- Most colonial families made their own furniture, clothes, and tools.

- There were many jobs in towns. Bakers, cooks, wigmakers, watchmakers, bricklayers, gun makers, and ministers were just a few.

- When people got sick there were no trained doctors.

- Most illness was treated at home or by the town barber.

- Barbers cut hair, "bled people," and pulled teeth.

- Colonial towns were dirty and smelled bad.

- Many people got sick because they lived with dirt, rats, and other pests!

- Music was enjoyed by colonists.

- Most people knew many songs and could play one or more instruments.

- Colonists also played games such as cards and marbles.

Doing Division

Springboard:

Students should complete the "What Do You Think?" handout.
(Any divisions are fine as long as students justify their ideas.)

Objective: The student will be able to describe regional differences between the New England, Middle and Southern colonies.

Materials:
What Do You Think? (Springboard handout)
Comparing Colonial Regions (handout)
Who Am I? - Rules of the Game (handout or transparency)
index cards or slips of paper

Terms to know:
region - area with common economic activity, lifestyle, physical features, etc.
climate - the normal weather in a place
port - place for ships to dock
piedmont - rolling land at the bottom of mountains
industry - businesses that do the same things

Procedure:

- After student(s) share their Springboard divisions, explain that *in this lesson the student(s) will learn about the three regions in Colonial America.* (**NOTE**: Students should adjust their maps as needed to show the three divisions "historians" use regarding the American colonies: New England Colonies (Massachusetts, Rhode Island, Connecticut and New Hampshire); the Middle Colonies (New York, Pennsylvania, New Jersey and Delaware); and the Southern Colonies (Virginia, Maryland, North and South Carolina and Georgia).

- Distribute "Comparing Colonial Regions" and distribute or display the rules of the game and review. **For group instruction** arrange students in groups of 4 or 5. Have the groups use index cards or slips of paper to write quotes of people from the three regions based on chart information. *(Example: A colonist from New England might say "Will this winter never end? We are going to run out of firewood, but we'll just get more from the forest.")* Each quote should end with the question "Who am I?" with the answer on the back of the card. **For individualized instruction** the student should prepare to play the game against the teacher/parent.

- Have the student(s) play the game according to the rules for as long as desired. Depending on student ability, the charts could be used for reference.

- Then lead a discussion, having the student(s) identify comparisons and contrasts between the three regions.

What Do YOU Think? ?

DIRECTIONS: Based on what you have learned so far in this unit, how could you divide the 13 colonies into **REGIONS** based on economics, way of life, land, etc. Color or shade the map to show your ideas. Then, explain your "regions" at right and below.

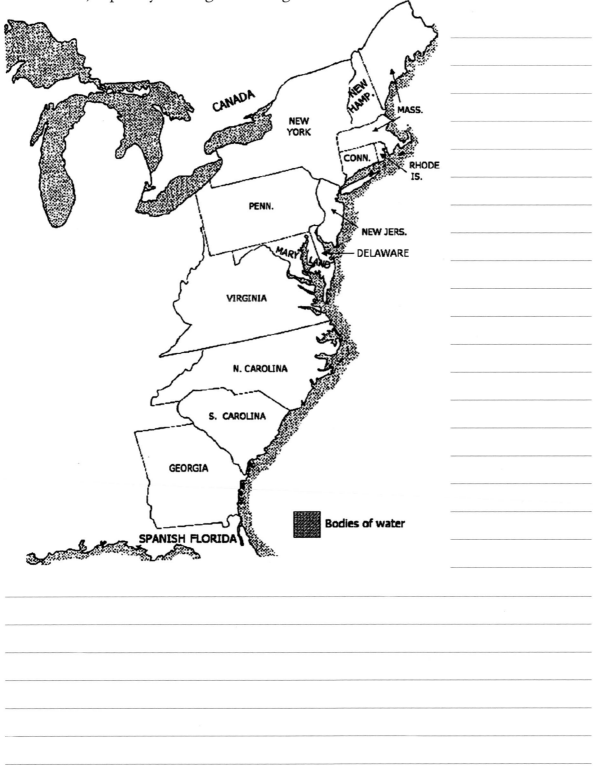

CANADA

NEW YORK

NEW HAMP.

MASS.

CONN.

RHODE IS.

PENN.

NEW JERS.

MARY LAND — DELAWARE

VIRGINIA

N. CAROLINA

S. CAROLINA

GEORGIA

SPANISH FLORIDA

■ Bodies of water

COMPARING COLONIAL REGIONS

	NEW ENGLAND	MIDDLE	SOUTH
COLONIES	· Massachusetts · Rhode Island · Connecticut · New Hampshire	· New York · Pennsylvania · New Jersey · Delaware	· Virginia · Maryland · North Carolina · South Carolina · Georgia
LAND	· Mountains · Boston Harbor and many other ports along the coast · Hilly and rocky	· Mountains · Ports and bays · Many deep, wide rivers	· Mountains · Good rivers and ports · Long coastline · Piedmont
CLIMATE	· Mild summers · Long, cold winters	· Not too hot, not too cold	· Mild, but sticky and hot
RESOURCES	· Forests (timber) · Close to water	· Good soil for farming · Close to water	· Good soil for farming
ECONOMY	· Fishing · Building ships · Trade · Small farms · Much industry	· Farming and raising animals · Some trade · Skilled crafts in homes (weavers, shoemakers, bakers, etc.)	· Large farms worked by slaves · Grew mainly cash crops (for money, such as tobacco)
WAY OF LIFE	· Mostly Puritans and other religious groups · Church was center of life	· People lived differently in different areas · Went to town - markets, stores, church, etc.	· A few port cities on the coast · Some large land owners · Others poor
OTHER	· Many large towns with schools, colleges, and shops · Many goods and services · Town meetings held for news and other information	· Mix of large cities, small villages, and farms · Some areas much like New England; others more like the South	· Everything based on slave labor · Few schools and cities · Grew tobacco, rice, and later cotton

WHO AM I? - RULES OF THE GAME

o Use the chart to write at least four quotes from each region. After each quote, write "Who Am I?" Then write the answer on the back of the card.

o Take turns picking another group (or player) to challenge. The team or player that challenges should read one of its quotes and ask "Who Am I?"

o The challenged team (or player) has 10 seconds (timed on a clock or count "one Mississippi, two Mississippi") to answer "New Englander" "Middle Colonist" or "Southerner."

o If the challenged team (or player) gives the correct answer, 10 points is earned. If not, the challenging team earns 15 points.

o Then the next team (or player) takes a turn, challenging another.

o No team (or player) may be challenged twice in row.

o Any team (or player) not challenged in five turns is given the next question.

o The team with the most points at the end of the game wins.

Help Wanted

Springboard:
The student should complete the "Help Wanted in the Colonies" brainstorm. *(Answers will vary but should be logical.)*

Objective: The student will be able to describe the various jobs available in the colonies.

Materials: Help Wanted in the Colonies (Springboard handout)
Jobs Cards (2 pages of card cut-outs)

Terms to know: **profession** - job
pewter - metal made from tin mixed with other metals

Procedure:

· After reviewing the Springboard, explain that *this lesson more closely examines the labor needed for each colonial region*.

· Student(s) can work individually, in pairs or small groups to sort the cards based on whether the job description would likely be for the New England, Middle or Southern colonies. (*Answers will vary somewhat but should reflect what they learned from the previous lesson.*)

· Then, have the groups re-sort the cards into skilled and unskilled labor. (*Answers will vary, but should be justified.*)

· Finally, have the groups re-sort the cards into who they think would be rich and poor. (*Answers will vary somewhat but will probably be similar groupings to the second sort.*)

· Then lead a discussion of the following questions:

  ? How do you think these jobs were filled in the colonies? (*Answers will vary, but many people came to the colonies to work!*)

  ? Based on these job opportunities, do you think people's lives improved by coming to the colonies? (*Answers will vary but there were many jobs available. Of course if a person didn't have needed skills, opportunities were more limited.*)

  ? Who could get rich by coming to the colonies? (*Answers may vary. Large landowners probably had the best chance, but others such as merchants, shopkeepers, and skilled craftspeople could also do well.*)

  ? How do you think the growing population would have affected jobs (*Some may argue that more people would mean fewer jobs available, while others may argue that more people would mean business was thriving and more workers were needed.*)

· Also during the discussion, have the student(s) share the professions of various characters in the books they are reading, the levels of skill required, and the prospects for "success."

HELP WANTED
in the Colonies

DIRECTIONS: Fill in the blanks with jobs that may have needed to be filled in the colonies. Think about both skilled and unskilled professions. These can be jobs in cities or towns, on farms, or in ports; in winter, spring, summer, or fall. They can be jobs done anywhere in any region of the colonies. Try to fill the whole page!

_____   _____

_____   _____

_____   _____

_____   _____

_____   _____

_____   _____

_____   _____

_____   _____

_____   _____

_____   _____

_____   _____

_____   _____

_____   _____

JOBS CARDS

BARBER Cut hair, shaved beards, and pulled teeth	**LOGGER** Worked in the forests cutting down and getting trees to mills
TEACHER Taught the children of rich families	**CABINET MAKER** Built wooden cabinets and shelves at home or in a town shop
MAID Cleaned and cared for homes of the rich families	**PREACHER** Preached on Sundays, performed marriages and funerals
WEAVER Worked in their homes weaving cotton into cloth	**COOK** Worked in the homes of the rich making all the meals
CARPENTER Built houses and other buildings	**MILL WORKER** Worked grinders to grind corn and wheat into flour
PLANTER Owned a lot of land and workers to plant crops	**BREECHES MAKER** Made men's pants
TOBACCO FARM WORKER Worked in the field pulling weeks and picking tobacco plants	**RIVER GUIDE / CAPTAIN** Used their boats to carry goods and people on the rivers
SHIP BUILDER Built and sold small and large boats	**GROOMER** Cared for horses
BAKER Made bread and other baked goods in town for sale	**WATCH MAKER** Made and repaired watches and clocks.
DOCK WORKER Loaded and unloaded ships coming into port	**MIDWIFE** Helped women have babies and worked as healers
GUNSMITH Made and fixed guns	**GARDENER** Planted, weeded and tended to vegetable gardens

SMALL FARMER Owned just enough land to feed one's family	**HOUSE SERVANT** Waited on members of rich families
WIG MAKER Made wigs for men and women and cut and styled hair	**PRINTER** Printed and sold newspapers and other writings
LAUNDRY WORKER Washed and ironed clothes for others	**DRIVER** Drove people, mostly the rich, in carriages
CUTLER Made, sharpened and repaired knives	**OVERSEER** Managed field workers and slaves
MERCHANT Trader who bought and sold goods from Europe or elsewhere	**FARMER** Planted and tended land to feed one's family and sell some crops
PEWTERER Made cups, teapots, candlesticks, and other things of pewter	**FISHERMAN** Caught fish either on their own or others' boats
RICE FIELD WORKER Planted, weeded, and picked rice for the land owner	**BOOK KEEPER** Kept track of sales and money for business owners
SHOP KEEPER Owned or worked in general store; sold food, cloth, and other goods	**VETERINARIAN** Treated sick horses and other animals
NURSEMAID Took care of the children of rich families	**APOTHECARY** Sold drugs (medicines) and chemicals
BRICK LAYER Worked on building sites	**STAY MAKER** Made under garments that pulled in women's waists to make them look thin
DELIVERY BOY Ran errands for people in town	**NAILOR** Cared for the teeth of a "card" used to prepare wool or cotton for weaving

Will Work for Tools

Springboard:
  Students should study "What is This?" and answer the title question.
  (Answer will vary; this is an advertisement for indentured servants.)

Objective: The student will be able to explain why people became indentured servants.

Materials: What is This? (Springboard handout)
                        Dear Mother and Father (2-page handout)
                        Pick a Position (handout)

Terms to know: **indentured servant** - a worker who works under a
                        master for a number of years for training, tools, etc.
                        contract - a legal agreement
                        passage - cost of a journey
                        apprentice - one who learns a skill from a master
                        trade - a skilled profession

Procedure:

- After reviewing the Springboard, explain that *in this lesson the student(s) will learn more about why people became indentured servants.*
- Distribute "Dear Mother and Father" and have the student(s) read the story individually or together, depending on student ability level. Encourage the student(s) to highlight or underline important passages.
- Then distribute "Pick a Position." The student(s) should chose one of the statements to write two to three paragraphs based on information from the lesson.
- Have them share their positions and ideas.
- **EXTENSION**: **For group instruction** hold a short debate. Divide students by the positions they took in the lesson. Each side should prepare an opening statement, at least three points to defend their position, and a closing statement. Then have each side take turns presenting their ideas and allowing responses (twice back and forth).

What Is This?

For freight or paſſage apply to Scot and Brown, merchants in Glaſgow, or Captain William M'Cunn, in Greenock.

WANTED,

To go to Virginia, under indentures for a few years, A Young Man, who underſtands LATIN GREEK, and MATHEMATICS, to ſerve as a Tutor in a gentleman's family.

A lad who has ſerved an appreticeſhip as a ſurgeon, to live with one of his own profeſſion.

Two Gardeners, who underſtands their buſineſs well, particularly the work in a garden,

Theſe, properly recommended, will meet with ſuitable encouragement, on applying to Buchanan and Simſon, merchants in Glaſgow.

THAT the FOGGAGE of the Laigh Park of Boogs, conſiſting of ſixty four acres, or there-by. is to be ſet till December next, and entered to

---

DIRECTIONS: Explain what you think this newspaper clipping is saying and why it was put in the paper.

_____

_____

_____

_____

_____

_____

_____

_____

Dear Mother and Father,

I am sure you must both be sick with worry. I know you have not heard from me in quite a time. I am writing now so you shall know what has gone on in these last months. When I went to London I found no work. The little money I brought was gone in no time. I was left living on the street, hungry and cold.

One night a well-dressed man offered to buy me a hot meal. His job was to sign up workers to go to the colonies. The man told me stories of the New World. He said he could arrange my indenture and find me work. He said I might even be able to own my own land one day! So I signed his contract straight away, with hope that I would never be hungry again!

He took me to a building at the dock. I was to wait there for the ship to take me to America. I told him I had no money. But he said "No matter," and paid for my passage. I waited with other men, women, and even some children for two days until the ship sailed.

I wish I could tell you that the journey was a good one. But in fact it was awful! They gave us hardly any food and kept us below the deck most of the time. It was dark and dirty there. I rarely even saw the sun for ten whole weeks. Sadly, a few on board died on the way.

We finally arrived in port on a Saturday at the Virginia colony. A few on the ship had masters waiting for them. They had their work arranged for before they left England. The rest of us had to wait until Tuesday to learn our fates.

There were some who were bought to be apprentices for all sorts of trades. They learn their work and can later find jobs after their indenture ends. I was not so lucky though. My new master is Mr. Jonas Croft, a tobacco planter to whom I am bound for six years. I must work his fields six days a week from dawn to dusk. Mr. Croft gives me clothes, food, and shelter but I have no freedom at all. I must ask to do anything. I may not leave his plantation. And I cannot even marry unless he approves. Still, I do have three meals a day and a bed. And that is more than I had before.

The overseer, Mr. Brown is a mean bloke. He yells and whips us. When I first worked in the fields, I would get sick from it. It is very hot here, not like England. I would have to stop work to drink water or catch my breath. For that Brown would whip me until I bled. I have even seen the brute whip women and poor children, too.

I know it sounds bad, but I don't want you to worry about me. My years of service will pass in short time. Then Mr. Croft will give me clothes, tools, seed, and 50 acres of my own land! That is far more than I could have dreamed of in England.

I know I can survive Mr. Brown, too. Six months have now passed. I just do my job and think of the time when I shall be free. 'Tis this hope that takes me through each day. I shall write again.

Your loving son,
James

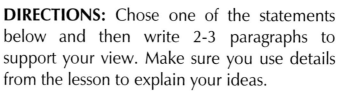 

Pick a Position!

DIRECTIONS: Chose one of the statements below and then write 2-3 paragraphs to support your view. Make sure you use details from the lesson to explain your ideas.

"Being an indentured servant was worth the hardship it caused."

"Becoming an indentured servant was a mistake for most people."

In Chains

Springboard:
  Students should study the "Triangular Trade" diagram and answer the questions.

Objective: The student will be able to explain the "need" for slavery and describe slave life in the American colonies.

Materials: Triangular Trade (Springboard handout)
                        Our Lives in Pictures (3-page handout)
                        Check It Off Your List (handout)

Terms to know: **diagram** - drawing to show how something works
                        inference - a logical idea based on knowledge

Procedure:

· After reviewing the Springboard, explain that *in this lesson the student(s) will learn more about why slaves were brought to the colonies and what their lives were like*.

· Distribute "Our Lives in Pictures." Have the student(s) study the pictures individually or in pairs and use the space provided to record what they see and learn about the slave trade and slavery in the colonies from the pictures.

· Have the student(s) share their ideas and discuss, using the answer page to prompt discussion as students fill in gaps in their answers.

· Then distribute "Check It Off Your List." Explain that *the student(s) should compare and contrast indentured servants and slaves by completing the checklist*. Go on to explain that *in some cases, they make have to make inferences* (review term).

· Have the student(s) share and compare their ideas and discuss. During the discussion have them summarize the similarities between indentured servants and slaves and highlight their main differences, including the role both played in colonial America. *(There was a great need for labor in the colonies so they could grow and thrive. Indentured servants and slaves were brought in to fill the need. Both came from other continents, lived hard lives with frequent punishment, and had little freedom. Indentured servants, however, eventually earned their freedom and the tools to start a new life.)*

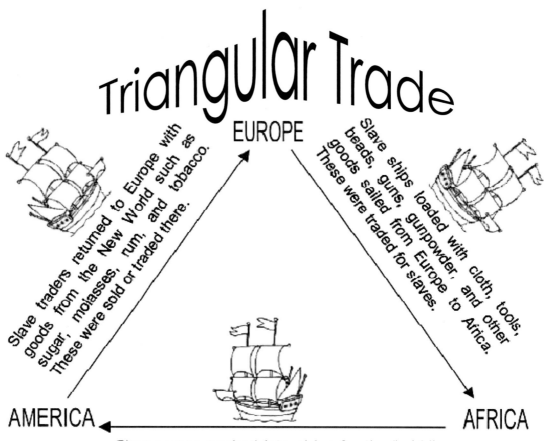

Triangular Trade

EUROPE

Slave traders returned to Europe with goods from the New World such as sugar, molasses, rum, and tobacco. These were sold or traded there.

Slave ships loaded with cloth, tools, beads, guns, gunpowder, and other goods sailed from Europe to Africa. These were traded for slaves.

AMERICA

AFRICA

Slaves were packed into ships for the "middle passage." The trip could last as long as ten weeks. Slaves were kept in chains, given little food or water. Many died along the way.

This graphic would **BEST** be called a
    A. chart.   B. graph.   C. map.   D. diagram.

Which of these is true according to the graphic?
    A. Africans bought slaves to send to Europe.
    B. European traders brought slaves to Africa.
    C. Slave traders exchanged goods for slaves.
    D. Tobacco and sugar were grown in Europe.

The best explanation for a triangle shaped graphic is because
    A. there were three locations involved.
    B. America and Africa are equal size.
    C. trade went in a clockwise direction.
    D. slaves were only found in Africa.

Explain why you think the trip from Africa was called the "middle passage?"

_____

_____

_____

_____

Triangular Trade
Answers & Explanations

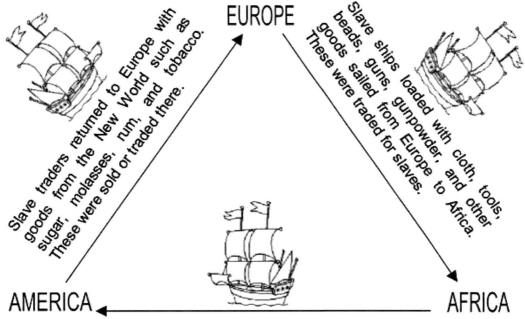

EUROPE

Slave traders returned to Europe with goods from the New World such as sugar, molasses, rum, and tobacco. These were sold or traded there.

Slave ships loaded with cloth, tools, beads, guns, gunpowder, and other goods sailed from Europe to Africa. These were traded for slaves.

AMERICA

AFRICA

Slaves were packed into ships for the "middle passage." The trip could last as long as ten weeks. Slaves were kept in chains, given little food or water. Many died along the way.

This graphic would **BEST** be called a
    A. chart.   B. graph.   C. map.   D. diagram. *
    (Introduce the term if students are unfamiliar with it.)

Which of these is true according to the graphic?   *(By studying the graphic*
    A. Africans bought slaves to send to Europe.   *students can see*
    B. European traders brought slaves to Africa.   *the other three*
    C. Slave traders exchanged goods for slaves. *   *choices are false.)*
    D. Tobacco and sugar were grown in Europe.

The best explanation for a triangle-shaped graphic is because   *(A triangle has three*
    A. there were three locations involved. *   *sides like the graphic.*
    B. America and Africa are equal size.   *Other choices are either*
    C. trade went in a clockwise direction.   *false or have nothing*
    D. slaves were only found in Africa.   *to do with triangles!)*

Explain why you think the trip from Africa was called the "middle passage?" *Answers will vary. Students should see that this leg of the journey was the second or middle step in the slave trade.*

OUR LIVES IN PICTURES

What can be learned?

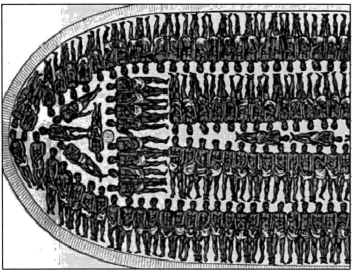

THE BREAKDOWN

OUR LIVES IN PICTURES
SUGGESTED ANSWERS & EXPLANATIONS

What Can Be Learned? *(in order as pictured)*

· *African slave traders raided villages to capture men, women, and children to sell or trade to the Europeans for guns, gunpowder, tools and other goods. Sometimes, African leaders sold prisoners of war, criminals, and others to the traders themselves. At times traders captured their own prisoners, but for the most part the trade was Africans capturing enemies or weaker people to increase their own strength. The guns they traded for made them more secure and less likely to fall prey to other traders.*

· *Once captured, the slaves were brought to prisons or trading posts to await being traded and sent to the Americas. Here they were kept in chains and given little food or water. They were strictly guarded by their African captors and then the white slave traders. These posts were located along the western coast of Africa. Few really understood what was happening to them or what their futures held; they only knew they were prisoners.*

· *Slaves left West Africa, crowded into ships for the voyage to the Americas. The trip lasted 8-12 weeks, during which the prisoners were often chained with little room to move. Though required to eat and drink to ensure the slavers' profits, both the food and living conditions were miserable. It was not uncommon for would-be slaves to jump overboard, if chance permitted.*

· *The "middle passage" resulted in the death of many, as the slaves were kept below decks for most of the trip. They had little fresh air, food, or water and were whipped or otherwise punished by the traders if they did anything wrong. Many died from disease and starvation.*

· *Once in the Americas, the slaves were auctioned like livestock. Would-be owners examined their teeth, skin, eyes, and so forth in deciding to bid. Families that may have remained together up to this time were usually split up as children were taken from their parents, never to see them again.*

· *Most slaves worked long, hot, grueling days in the fields. They were guarded and managed by white overseers, who used the whip and any other means to maximize their output.*

· *Some slaves worked as house servants or nursemaids, looking after the white children of their masters. House slaves tended to live better than field workers.*

· *Slaves who tried to escape or otherwise misbehaved were punished severely and often publicly to send a message to others who might consider leaving.*

· *Free time was spent with the other slaves and (if they were lucky) their families dancing, playing music and visiting. Unfortunately, though, there was little free time to enjoy such activities.*

Check It Off Your List! ✓

DIRECTIONS: For each statement, decide if it is true of an indentured servant, a slave, or both. Then check your answer in the box at right.

	SERVANT	SLAVE	BOTH
Sailed across the ocean			
Signed a contract			
Were sometimes parted from their families			
Some died from traveling			
Were sold by traders			
Had their passage paid for in exchange for work			
Could be free after a set number of years			
Were given food, shelter, and clothes			
Had a master			
Worked in the fields			
Had no freedom			
Given their own land at some point			
Were chained			
Could be beaten			
Worked as apprentices			
Were watched by overseers			
Came from Africa			
Some tried to run away			
Came from England			
May have been sorry to be in America			
Needed permission to do anything			
Made the decision to come to the New World			
Did not earn money			
Had little free time			
Could not leave the master's house or land			
Were sold to the highest bidder			
Were sold by their leaders			
Enjoyed music, dancing, and family time			
Could not go back to their homes			
Were brought to posts on the coastline			
Were captured and sold to traders			
Were held at docks waiting for ships.			
Often were whipped and punished			
Journey was called the "middle passage"			
Were traded for goods such as guns or tools			
Wanted a better life			
Could later work for money			
Needed for labor in the colonies			

Check It Off Your List!
Suggestions for Answers

NOTE: *These are only <u>suggestions</u> for answers. Students may have other ideas which are fine, if reasonable and justified.*

	SERVANT	SLAVE	BOTH
Sailed across the ocean			X
Signed a contract	X		
Were sometimes parted from their families			X
Some died from traveling			X
Were sold by traders		X	
Had their passage paid for in exchange for work	X		
Could be free after a set number of years	X		
Were given food, shelter, and clothes			X
Had a master			X
Worked in the fields			X
Had no freedom			X
Given their own land at some point	X		
Were chained		X	
Could be beaten			X
Worked as apprentices	X		
Were watched by overseers			X
Came from Africa		X	
Some tried to run away			X
Came from England	X		
May have been sorry to be in America			X
Needed permission to do anything			X
Made the decision to come to the New World	X		
Did not earn money			X
Had little free time			X
Could not leave the master's house or land			X
Were sold to the highest bidder		X	
Were sold by their leaders		X	
Enjoyed music, dancing, and family time			X
Could not go back to their homes		X	
Were brought to posts on the coastline			X
Were captured and sold to traders		X	
Were held at docks waiting for ships.			X
Often were whipped and punished			X
Journey was called the "middle passage"		X	
Were traded for goods such as guns or tools		X	
Wanted a better life	X		
Could later work for money	X		
Needed for labor in the colonies			X

In Control!

Springboard:
    Students should read "Mercantilism" and answer the questions.

Objective: The student will be able to explain mercantilism and how it affected the colonies.

Materials: Mercantilism (Springboard handout)
                        Cause & Effects (handout)

Terms to know: **mercantilism** - the idea that a country's power comes from their wealth
                        tax - money paid to a government

Procedure:

·   After reviewing the Springboard, explain that _England had a policy of mercantilism in regards to its American colonies_. Go on to explain that _in this lesson the student(s) will analyze the effects of English mercantilism_.

·   Distribute the "Cause & Effects" handout. The student(s) should work individually, in pairs, or small groups to examine the various characteristics and actions involved in English mercantilism and predict the effects and problems that may have resulted.

·   Have the student(s) share and compare their ideas and discuss. (*Answers will vary, but should reflect the idea that while controlling colonies and other mercantilist polices brings wealth, the laws and other means of control can also cause tension in the colonies and have negative effects on others.*)

MERCANTILI$M

    Mercantilism is the idea that a nation must be rich to be strong. Countries grew rich by owning colonies. The colonies gave them raw materials and resources. They also offered a place to trade goods and they bought products from Europe.

    To make this system work, the mother country had to have strict control. For example, the British East India Company was the only trading firm allowed to trade with the British colonies. Of course, the company had to share its earnings with England

    The British <u>crown</u> also controlled the colonies' resources. Raw materials, such as wood, were shipped from the colonies to England. There the wood was made into furniture, paper, and other goods. Then, these items were sent back to the colonies for colonists to buy. Another way the mother land made money was to tax its colonies. They charged fees for everything from tea to stamps.

    Colonies could make a nation rich. European powers would compete to gain control of as much land as they could. Each country wanted to own more and more colonies to grow richer and richer. This led to tensions and even wars between some countries.

Which definition **<u>BEST FITS</u>** the use of the word "crown" in the reading?
-    A. the top of a head
-    B. a king or queen
-    C. a golden hat
-    D. part of a tooth

Which **<u>SYNONYMS</u>** were used in the reading?
-    A. mercantilism / strong
-    B. resources / furniture
-    C. country / nation
-    D. trade / earnings

Find one more pair of words that are synonyms: _____

The main idea of the passage is
-    A. Great Britain made money from its colonies.
-    B. A colony's trade was controlled by a mother country.
-    C. Owning colonies was important to mercantilism.
-    D. The American colonies had many raw materials to use.

Do you think on the whole mercantilism was good or bad? Explain your ideas.

_____

_____

_____

_____

MERCANTILI$M - AN$WER$ & EXPLANATION$

Mercantilism is the idea that a nation must be rich to be strong. Countries grew rich by owning colonies. The colonies gave them raw materials and resources. They also offered a place to trade goods and they bought products from Europe.

To make this system work, the mother country had to have strict control. For example, the British East India Company was the only trading firm allowed to trade with the British colonies. Of course, the company had to share its earnings with England

The British <u>crown</u> also controlled the colonies' resources. Raw materials, such as wood, were shipped from the colonies to England. There the wood was made into furniture, paper, and other goods. Then, these items were sent back to the colonies for colonists to buy. Another way the mother land made money was to tax its colonies. They charged fees for everything from tea to stamps.

Colonies could make a nation rich. European powers would compete to gain control of as much land as they could. Each country wanted to own more and more colonies to grow richer and richer. This led to tensions and even wars between some countries.

Which definition **BEST FITS** the use of the word "crown" in the reading?
  A. the top of a head   C. a golden hat
  B. a king or queen *   D. part of a tooth
  (Students should approach these kinds of questions by substituting each phrase into the sentence. In this case, the only answer that makes sense is B.)

Which **SYNONYMS** were used in the reading?
  A. mercantilism / strong   C. country / nation *
  B. resources / furniture   D. trade / earnings

Find one more pair of words that are synonyms: *Possibilities include: resources & raw materials – while not exact, the two are often used interchangeably; company & firm; power & control; England & Britain; taxes & fees; country & land; etc.*

The main idea of the passage is
  A. Great Britain made money from its colonies.
  B. A colony's trade was controlled by a mother country.
  C. Owning colonies was important to mercantilism.*
  D. The American colonies had many raw materials to use.
  (Most of the passage talks about how colonies are the key to mercantilism. The other choices, while true, are details supporting choice C.)

Do you think on the whole mercantilism was good or bad? Explain your ideas. *Answers may vary but should be well-explained. It could be seen as positive, at least to wealthy countries that become more powerful. Some may argue it is wrong to take advantage of others' lands, resources, and people or that the competition mercantilism sparked resulted in wars.*

►CAUSE & EFFECTS➤

DIRECTIONS: Read all the ways that mercantilism played out in the American colonies. Then predict at least one **EFFECT** of each: on the mother country and on the American colonists.

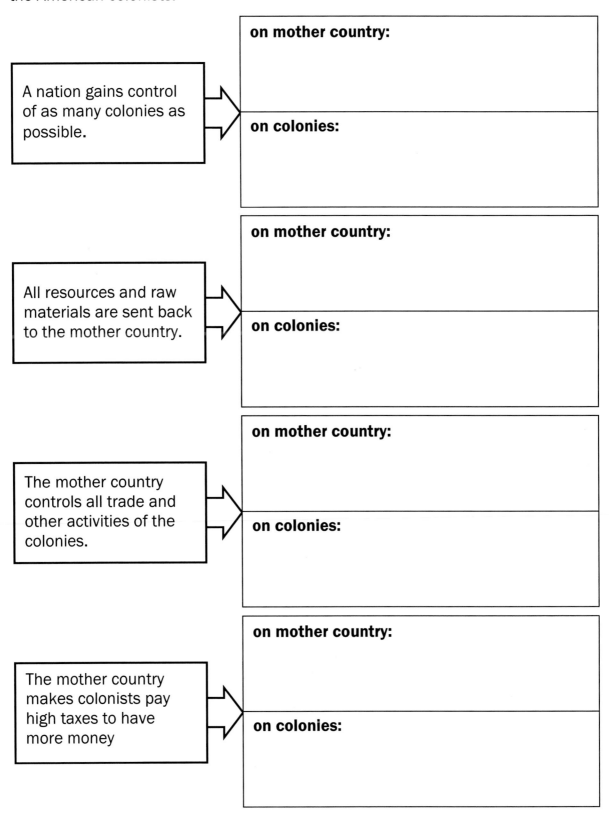

A nation gains control of as many colonies as possible.

on mother country:

on colonies:

All resources and raw materials are sent back to the mother country.

on mother country:

on colonies:

The mother country controls all trade and other activities of the colonies.

on mother country:

on colonies:

The mother country makes colonists pay high taxes to have more money

on mother country:

on colonies:

Rivals

Objective: The student will be able to explain the causes and outcomes of the French and Indian War.

Materials: "_____" (Springboard handout)
                A Tale of Two Sides (2 page handout)
                Webbing the War (handout)

Terms to know: **retreat** - to run away or move back
                allies - people or groups that join and work together for a common goal

Procedure:

·   After reviewing the Springboard, explain that _the treaty ending King George's War did not settle the issues between the French and English. The two countries went to war once again in 1754 in what would be called The French and Indian War_. Go on to explain that _this lesson examines the issues that caused this war._

·   Distribute "A Tale of Two Sides" and "Webbing the War." Have student(s) read the narratives individually or in pairs and complete their webs. (**NOTE:** Depending on student ability, you can suggest categories such as "who, what, where, when and why" or "causes, important people, important factors, important places, outcomes," etc. to examine.)

·   Have the student(s) share their webs and add information as needed. Explain that _England won the war and ended French influence in the American colonies. However England lost many soldiers and spent a huge amount of money to fight the war_.

1066	Normans from France conquer England
1242	Saintonge War; English and French knights go to war over land
1324	War of Saint - Sardos; France and England fight over land
1337	100 Years War; England tries to take over France
1689	King William's War; England and France fight over land in the New World
1702	St. Anne's War; England and France fight over forts in the New World
1745	King George's War; England captures fort from France
1756	Seven Years War; England wins Canada from the French

The best title for this graphic is
    A. "Conflict in the New World"
    B. "England versus France"
    C. "Wars from 1066 - 1756"
    D. "The Struggle for Control"

This graphic would **BEST** be described as a
    A. chart.   B. history.   C. timeline.   D. list.

Which sentence is **TRUE** based on the information given?
    A. St. Anne's War was fought shortly after King George's War.
    B. The 100 Years War and Seven Years War were 200 years apart.
    C. The first war between England and France was around 1242.
    D. King William's and St. Anne's Wars were fought within 15 years.

The wars shown were fought mostly over
    A. land.   B. forts.   C. the New World.   D. religion.

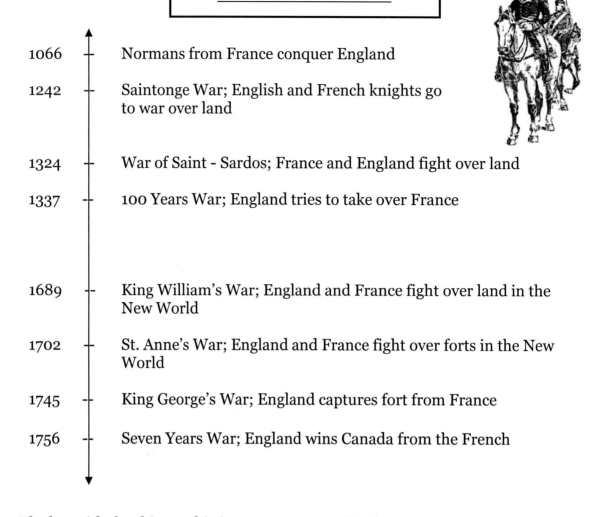

1066	Normans from France conquer England
1242	Saintonge War; English and French knights go to war over land
1324	War of Saint - Sardos; France and England fight over land
1337	100 Years War; England tries to take over France
1689	King William's War; England and France fight over land in the New World
1702	St. Anne's War; England and France fight over forts in the New World
1745	King George's War; England captures fort from France
1756	Seven Years War; England wins Canada from the French

The best title for this graphic is
    A. "Conflict in the New World"
    B. "England versus France" *
    C. "Wars from 1066 - 1756"
    D. "The Struggle for Control"

(Choice B alone applies to every event on the timeline. Students may want to choose C, but it is too broad. It is probable that nations other than England and France fought in that time.)

This graphic would **BEST** be described as a
    A. chart.   B. history.   C. timeline. *   D. list.
(Most students should know this. If not, point out the line.)

Which sentence is **TRUE** based on the information given?
    A. St. Anne's War was fought shortly after King George's War.
    B. The 100 Years War and Seven Years War were 200 years apart.
    C. The first war between England and France was around 1242.
    D. King William's and St. Anne's Wars were fought within 15 years. *
(Choices A, B and C are all FALSE according to timeline information.)

The wars shown were fought mostly over
    A. land*   B. forts   C. the New World   D. religion
(Although B and C are mentioned, "land" applies to both of these. Choice D not mentioned at all in the timeline.)

A Tale of Two Sides

His Highness King Louis,

As you well know, in 1752 we held all land west of the 13 British colonies and all Canada. Yet it was clear the Brits had their eye on our lands. So we built forts to protect our holdings. The best known of these forts was Fort Duquesne. It was very important since it was on the Ohio River. French fur traders needed control of the river for trade with the Native people. But British moving into the area caused this war.

For the first few years, we saw much success. We held Fort Duquesne and even captured the British Fort Necessity and others. We drove the Brits to retreat over and over. I think they thought this war would be easy. They had far more troops, but we have our secret weapon! The Native people are our allies! We have traded with them for years. But the filthy Brits steal their land. With the Natives' help it is but a matter of time before we shall win this war.

Louis—Joseph de Montcalm
French Commander

His Highness King George,

In 1753 I learned that the French had built a fort on the Ohio River. The fort was on land we had claimed. In fact the Ohio Company had even built settlements there. We need that land so we, too, can trade for furs with the Natives. Yet the French claimed this land as theirs! Hah! And they think their forts will scare us. I can promise His Highness there is no chance of that!

I sent the young Colonel George Washington with a message. He warned the French to leave the area. But they refused to leave! Stronger action had to be taken so I ordered Washington to run the French out of Fort Duquesne. In this, I am sad to say, the young man failed. Washington and his men were forced to retreat. Still, he built a new fort named Necessity nearby. He will soon try again, I know.

Robert Dinwiddle
Governor of Virginia

A Tale of Two Sides

Governor Dinwiddie,

    I am sorry to report that our next effort to take Fort Duquesne has failed as did the first. In fact the French also ran us from Fort Necessity! The war thus far has been awful, not at all what we might expect.

    Though my men have fought bravely, I fear our style of fighting is part of the problem. As you well know, we have always marched in neat rows toward the enemy. But the French and their Native allies do not face us to fight. They hide in bushes and behind rocks! This makes us fair targets, and we must retreat. Just today we were marching on the road and were shot at! This way of fighting is why we have lost battles, though we have more men. We have lost too many and continue to see defeats. Something must change, Sir.

                    Major George Washington
                    British Officer

His Highness King George,

    In 1757 it seemed as if we would lose this American war. It was then you asked me to take change. The plan I worked out had three parts. First, I changed the leaders of the troops in the field. One of the few I kept was George Washington. Though he failed in the first battles, he proved to be a great leader. I also sent Major General Jeffrey Archer to take command of the army.

    Second, I moved our forces into Canada. The goal was to cut off the French supply lines. We did that and were able to take control of the rivers as well. After that things went better.

    Last, I ordered our leaders to make peace with the Indians. They explained how it is better to side with us than the French. We have the power to help them. And so with Native help we have been able to turn things around. We took Fort Duquesne in 1758. I am honored to say the fort was renamed Pittsburg after me of course! The war, Your Highness, is now ended.

                    William Pitt the Elder
                    British Prime Minister

Webbing the War

DIRECTIONS: Use information from the story to complete the web. Each circle should be a category. Then jot notes about each one around the appropriate circle.

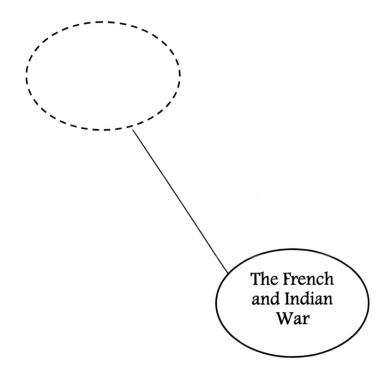

The French and Indian War

The Brewing Storm

Objective: The student will be able to explain England's actions after the French and Indian War.

Materials: By the End of the War… (Springboard handout)
                    Follow the Guide … (handout)
                    Meeting with King George (3-page handout)

Terms to know: **Parliament** - law makers in England

Procedure:

- After reviewing the Springboard, explain that *this lesson examines what King George did in an attempt to get England out of debt after the French and Indian War.*
- Distribute "Follow the Guide…" and "Meeting with King George." Explain that *the student(s) will read the play following the reading guide.* (As they read, they should read and stop as instructed, answering the questions as indicated on the guided reading form.) Have the student(s) read the play as directed individually or in groups.
- Then have them share their answers and discuss what they predicted would happen compared to what actually occurred. (*Answers will vary but should be well reasoned and justified.*) During the discussion, explain that *King George and Parliament did in fact go on to pass the laws discussed in the play and others. These laws would become part of a series of events that would eventually lead to the American Revolution.*

By the End of the War...

1. England gained control of all land to the Mississippi River and moved into Canada. Colonists could now move west.

2. The colonists felt safer with the French and Indians defeated.

3. England saw the colonies as even more valuable, as they were growing and doing well.

4. The population grew in the colonies. And it began to spread out more.

5. Education, art, and writing became more important in the colonies.

6. Many colonists learned to be good soldiers during the war.

7. The colonial governments had to make many decisions during the war. Then they didn't want to give up that power.

8. England was deeply in debt from fighting the war.

9. Many people died fighting the French and Indian War.

10. The colonists felt more able to care for themselves. They were proud of winning the war. They were ready to defend themselves.

What do you think was the **BEST** outcome of the French and Indian War? Why? _____

_____

_____

_____

_____

What do you think was the **WORST** outcome of the French and Indian War? Why? _____

_____

_____

_____

_____

Meeting With King George

Parts:
Walter Stuart, advisor to the king
King George III of England
Thomas Hutchins, economic advisor
William Banks, member of Parliament

Scene I

Stuart: Good evening My Lord. Have you have heard the news?

George: Yes, I just heard. This awful war has ended at last, and we have won!

Stuart: Not only that, Your Highness, but we now have many new chances to gain from the colonies.

George: Do you mean the land we took over? England is now the most powerful nation in the world. We now have more colonies than ever -- in America, Africa, India, and the Middle East!

Stuart: Yes, that is true, Sire. But I was thinking about all the money they can earn for you and England.

George: Of course I have thought about that! Do you think me a fool? I was not born yesterday! Everyone knows more colonies mean more money! It is simple mercantilism.

Stuart: Forgive me, Your Highness. It is just that now more than ever, we must work to make money for England.

George: Why now more than ever?

Stuart: My Lord, the war in the colonies has cost us dearly. Now, because of the American colonies, we are deeply in debt. We owe almost 133 million pounds!

George: 133 million you say? That's more than twice what we owed before their war. Then, Walter, you are right. We must make a plan as to what to do. We must pay this debt to keep England strong.

Stuart: Yes Sire, I shall go and speak with the other advisors at once.

Scene II

Stuart: My lord, your economic advisor is here to see you. I spoke with him. He has some thoughts to share with you.

George: Then bring him in at once!

©InspirEd Educators, Inc.

Hutchins:	Good evening, Your Highness. Thank you for seeing me. Walter and I spoke of this debt problem and think we have a plan.
George:	Do tell then.
Hutchins:	Sire, I think you should tax all British citizens.
George:	Hmmm. Interesting idea, but why ALL citizens? Why not just the colonists? Our great debt is due in large part to them.
Hutchins:	Please forgive me, Sire, but would not that be unfair?
George:	Unfair! I'll tell you what's unfair! We are 133 million pounds in debt due to THEIR war! We spent great sums to protect THEM! We sent soldiers; we built forts; and they hardly helped!
Hutchins:	What do you mean? Did they not aid the fight to rid their own lands of the French?
Stuart:	Some colonies did not send any troops at all! They SAID their men were needed to protect their own lands. Yet the same could be said of England. We were fighting elsewhere in the world, but we still sent troops to aid the American colonists!
George:	Can you believe how selfish those people are?!
Hutchins:	Sire, I am most sorry. I did not know about this. In view of these facts, it seems only fair to tax the colonists. They owe US a debt!
George:	I agree. 'Tis time to lay down the law. We have let these hangers-on get away with too much for too long.
Stuart:	I also could not agree more, Your Highness. While we face huge economic problems, they are doing quite well! They cheat you of what should be your share!
George:	Indeed. Walter, Thomas, I want you to go to Parliament at once. I want new tax laws passed straight away.
Hutchins:	Yes, Your Highness. It shall be done.

Scene III

Stuart:	Sire, William Banks is here to see you.
George:	William, what have you and Parliament come up with?
Banks:	Sire, we have a few ideas. First, what do you think of taxing sugar and other British goods going to the colonies? Taxing goods they

need and want is a simple way for them to repay you and England for all that has been done for them.

George: Quite true! And they cannot get those things from elsewhere. They shall have no choice but to pay our taxes. And what about tea? They are English. All English love tea.

Banks: A fine idea! We could even pass a law that they can only buy their tea from the British East India Company. Of course one hand washes the other with that firm.

George: And the colonists will surely not stop drinking tea. What else could we tax?

Banks: How about mail and paper?

George: Of course! Mail must have stamps! We shall charge fees for them.

Banks: In fact we could say that all printed materials must have a stamp!

George: Brilliant!

Stuart: Sire, we also have some ideas to save England money.

Banks: This is true, Your Highness. We thought of a law that colonists must house and feed our soldiers when in America.

George: Perfect! That is one cost we shall no longer have to pay. Such a law could save quite a bit of money!

Stuart: One last thing, Sire. I think we need to do something about the colonial governments. Some tend to ignore our laws. They think they can govern themselves!

George: This is true. They are surely growing too strong. What do you have in mind?

Banks: We think that from now on, all their laws should have to be approved by Parliament. In that way we can keep a close eye on them. Of course it goes without saying; we shall not approve any laws that do not serve in England's favor.

George: Men, I am most pleased with your ideas. Now, Parliament must begin at once. I should like to see some new laws on the books quite soon.

Banks: Yes, Sire. It shall be done.

FOLLOW THE GUIDE...

Read the list of parts in the play...
Based on the people, what do you think this play is about?

_____

_____

_____

Read Scene One...
Why do you think the French and Indian war was so costly? _____

_____

_____

_____

What do you think the king's advisors might tell him to do? _____

_____

_____

_____

Read Scene Two...
Do you agree with King George's thoughts on the colonists? Explain.

_____

_____

_____

Had you been a colonist, what would you have said to the king? _____

_____

_____

_____

Read Scene Three...
Which "idea" do you think will anger the colonists the most? Why?

_____

_____

_____

Predict three things you think might happen next. _____

_____

_____

_____

Close the Book on the Subject

Springboard:
Students should complete the "Character Close-Up" handout.
(Answers will vary.)

Objective: The student will compare and contrast events and people from their books to unit study.

Materials: Character Close-Up (Springboard handout)
                          Fact or Fiction? (handout - See NOTE)

Procedure:

- Have the student(s) share their questions and answers and explain that *they will be looking closely at the book they read during the unit to complete a project*.

- **NOTE:** Before copying and distributing the project handout, fill in the blanks with how many comparisons and contrasts you will require.

- Hand out "Fact or Fiction" and review the project requirements. If student(s) read the same books, they can complete the project in groups if desired. Some additional research may be required about topics in their books that may not have been studied in the unit.

- Have the student(s) present and evaluate their projects. Have them further practice their compare and contrast skills by comparing and contrasting books they read (if they read different ones).

©InspirEd Educators, Inc.

CHARACTER CLOSE-UP

DIRECTIONS: If you could meet your favorite character in the book you read, what questions would you ask? Write **5** and tell how you think he/she would answer.

QUESTION 1: _____

_____

ANSWER: _____

_____

QUESTION 2: _____

_____

ANSWER: _____

_____

QUESTION 3: _____

_____

ANSWER: _____

_____

QUESTION 4: _____

_____

ANSWER: _____

_____

QUESTION 5: _____

_____

ANSWER: _____

_____

Fact or Fiction?

For this project you will compare and contrast your book with real events and people in America's colonies. You should consider what you learned in this unit and compare/contrast that with the people and actions in your book. You should find at least _____ comparisons and _____ contrasts between book and study.

How you present your work is up to you, but it must be big enough to share (not just on a piece of paper). You may present your comparisons/contrasts one at a time (such as in a flip book) or all together (using a poster, illustrated Venn diagram, two-sided chart, etc.) Any format ideas are fine as long as you follow the guidelines.

But no matter WHAT you do, be

neat and creative!

Grade Your Work

Use this point scale to rate your work:
4 - Excellent   3 - Good   2 - Fair   1 - Poor   0 - Unacceptable

	Student:	Teacher:
Comparisons/contrasts	_____	_____
Ideas clearly explained	_____	_____
Easy to understand	_____	_____
Followed directions	_____	_____
Neat and creative	_____	_____

GRADE:

COMMENTS:

REVIEWING TERMS

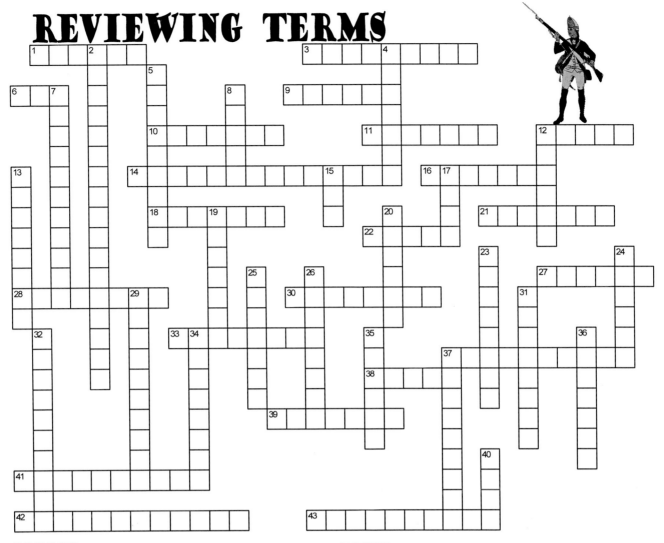

ACROSS:

1 those working together for a cause
3 family members in the past
6 enemy
9 church leader
10 money and business
11 illness
12 ranking among others
14 one who speaks and acts for others
16 daily log
18 agreement
21 one who starts something
22 soft, wet lowland
27 metal made from tin
28 a legal agreement
30 guarded town
33 rolling land near mountains
37 job
38 skilled profession
39 run away
41 one sent to spread religion
42 idea that power comes from colonies
43 English law makers

DOWN:

2 works for a master for passage, etc.
4 work with no product
5 an answer based on logic
7 travel to discover places
8 things bought and sold
12 land settled and ruled by another
13 things in nature that are useful
15 fees paid to the government
17 serious public promise
19 cost of a journey
20 sell
23 set of acts in respect or prayer
24 area with things in common
25 normal weather
26 way things differ
29 way things are alike
31 leader of a colony
32 one who learns a skill
34 business
35 ceremony
36 shows how something works
37 poor treatment of a person or group
40 place for ships to load and unload

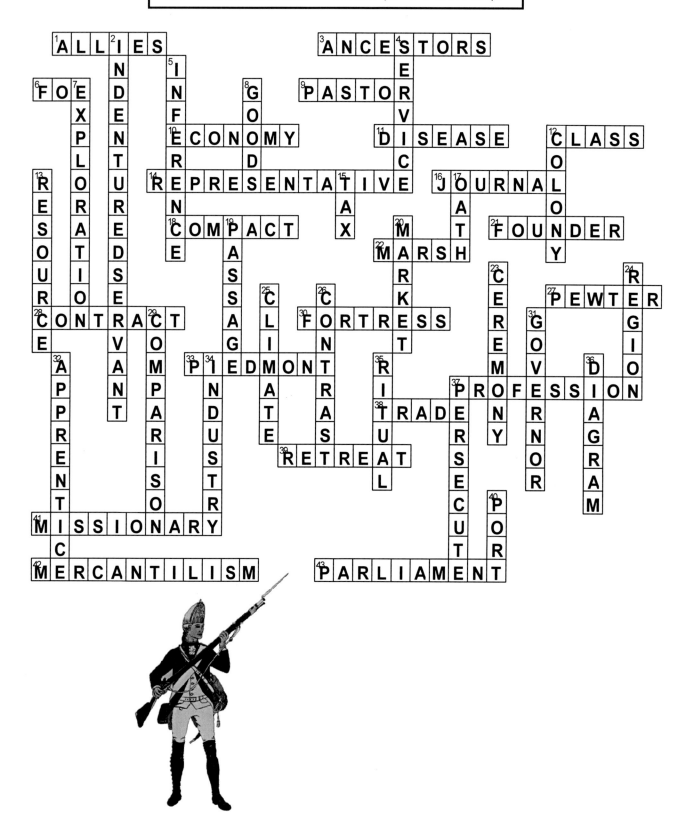

Matching - Write the letter of the correct answer in the blank:

_____	1. exploration	A. city protected by walls
_____	2. marsh	B. one who is sent to spread religion
_____	3. missionary	C. one learning a trade
_____	4. pastor	D. travel to discover new lands
_____	5. comparison	E. rolling land at the bottom of mountains
_____	6. piedmont	F. cost of a journey
_____	7. retreat	G. church leader
_____	8. fortress	H. run away or move back
_____	9. passage	I. ways that two things are alike
_____	10. apprentice	J. low, soft, wet land

Give an example of each of these:

11. good - _____

12. colony - _____

13. climate - _____

14. resource - _____

15. tax - _____

Multiple Choice - Write the letter of the correct answer in the blank:

_____ 16. The first **LASTING** English settlement in the New World was at
  A. Roanoke   B. Jamestown   C. St. Augustine   D. Plymouth

_____ 17. Which is the **LEAST** important reason people to come to the colonies?
  A. economic opportunities.   C. adventure.
  B. religious freedom.   D. mercantilism

_____ 18. The three main regions of Colonial America are called the
  A. New England, Middle, and Southern colonies.
  B. Western, Canadian, and American nations.
  C. French, English, and Native American lands.
  D. Northern, Eastern, and Southern countries.

_____ 19. The idea that a nation's power comes from its wealth is
  A. economics.   C. inferences.
  B. colonialism.   D. mercantilism.

Fully answer the following question:

20. Explain one way indentured servants and slaves were alike, and one way they differed.

The first winter in the New World was very hard for the Pilgrims. It was deathly cold and snowed heavily. The weather made it hard to build good shelters. Things improved by the spring, but less than half the colonists lived to see it. Still the Pilgrims met a Native American who helped them greatly.

Squanto taught the colonists how to get food from trees and plants. He taught them how to plant corn and other crops. By October the Pilgrims had **harvested** large amounts of corn, fruits, and vegetables. They even had enough to store for the winter. The Pilgrims were very thankful to Squanto for all his help. In fact the governor of the colony even declared a day of thanksgiving. The Pilgrims and Native Americans gathered for three days to eat, play games, run races, and play drums to celebrate.

_____ 21. The word "harvested" in the reading **MOST NEARLY** means
    A. planted.   B. burned.   C. gathered.   D. eaten.

_____ 22. The best choice for a title to this reading would be
    A. "A Long, First Winter."   C. "Better Times in Spring."
    B. "The First Thanksgiving."   D. "Learning from Mistakes."

_____ 23. One **CONTRAST** between Thanksgiving then and now would be
    A. both were to celebrate the harvest.
    B. feasts are eaten and include turkey.
    C. it took place in the spring at that time.
    D. the first event lasted three days, not one.

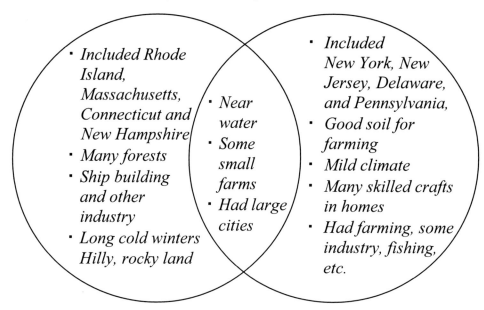

_____ 24. This graphic is called a
    A. Venn diagram.   B. bar graph.   C. pie chart.   D. mind map.

_____ 25. The information in the middle of the circles represents
    A. the New England Colonies.   C. comparisons between the two.
    B. contrasts between two regions.   D. the Middle Colonies.

America's Colonies (B)

Fill in the blanks with unit terms:

1. Many Natives died from the _____ they caught from the colonists.
2. The king named a _____ to lead each of the colonies.
3. A/An _____ is a serious promise often made in front of others.
4. The man heard a noise and called, "Who goes there, friend or _____?"
5. The Church of England would _____ people of other religions.
6. The servant's_____ to America was paid by his master.
7. The _____ learned the skills of his trade from a master.
8. The fierce attack forced the French soldiers to _____ to their fort.
9. The _____ was sent to teach his religion to the natives.
10. Kings in Europe paid for _____ of America to claim colonies.

Give an example of each of these:

11. climate - _____
12. fortress - _____
13. founder - _____
14. service - _____
15. profession - _____

Multiple Choice - Write the letter of the correct answer in the blank:

_____ 16. Which of these statements is **<u>TRUE</u>** about indentured servants?
    A. Some were brought to the colonies by slave traders.
    B. They lived easy, comfortable lives in the New World.
    C. Most ran away from their masters once in America.
    D. They worked for a few years; then earned their freedom.

_____ 17. Which of these places is **<u>NOT</u>** the name of a colonial American region?
    A. Northern   B. New England   C. Middle   D. Southern

_____ 18. Which reason for colonists coming to America was **<u>LEAST</u>** important?
    A. religious freedom   C. economic opportunity
    B. a better life   D. to help the king

_____ 19. Mercantilism is the idea that
    A. traders are more valuable than farmers.
    B. a nation's power comes from wealth.
    C. colonies must be near water for trade.
    D. resources should be shared by all.

Fully answer the following question on your own paper and attach:

20. Explain at least one reason for the French and Indian War and one outcome of the war.

America's Colonies (C)

Fill in the blanks with unit terms:

1. An oath is to spoken, as a/an _____ is to written.
2. Tin is to all the same metal, as _____ is to tin in a mixture.
3. Houses are to homes, as products are to _____.
4. A parking lot is to cars, as a/an _____ is to ships.
5. A student is to a teacher, as a/an _____ is to a skilled master.
6. Book is to product, as teaching is to _____.
7. Come is to go, as advance is to _____.
8. The inventor is to a new machine, as the _____ was to a new colony.
9. A school teacher is the three R's, as a/an _____ is to religion.
10. Friend is to ally, as enemy is to _____.

Use unit terms to name each grouping:

11. mother countries, colonies, wealth - _____
12. cold, mild, tropical, dry - _____
13. wet, coastal, soft ground, grasses - _____
14. rich, poor, middle, slave - _____
15. England, lawmaking, Upper and Lower Houses - _____

Multiple Choice - Write the letter of the correct answer in the blank:

_____ 16. Which sentence **CONTRASTS** slaves and indentured servants?
   A They had hard lives and could be beaten for small mistakes.
   B. Slaves had masters but indentured servants were free.
   C. They both had their passages to America paid by others.
   D. Indentured servants were eventually free to leave.

_____ 17. Which sentence is a **COMPARISON** between England and its colonies?
   A. People in England and its colonies obeyed the same king's law.
   B. All in England and its colonies could practice their religions freely.
   C. Life was much harder for people in England than in the Americas.
   D. England had no resources of its own and had to rely on its colonies.

_____ 18. The ____ colonies had more industry, while the ___ had bigger farms.
   A. Southern … New England   C. Northern … Middle
   B. New England … Southern   D. Middle … Northern

_____ 19. Which factor is **LEAST** involved in the economy of a region?
   A. money   B. trade   C. schools   D. farms

Fully answer the following question on your own paper and attach:

20. What do you think led the **MOST** colonists to come to America? Explain.

Form A:

1. D
2. J
3. B
4. G
5. I
6. E
7. H
8. A
9. F
10. C

11. tea, cloth, sugar, etc.
12. Jamestown, Plymouth, Massachusetts, Virginia, etc.
13. warm, mild, cold, wet, etc.
14. timber, gold, minerals, water, etc.
15. sugar, tea, income, sales, etc.
16. B
17. D
18. A
19. D
20. Both worked hard, had masters, lacked freedom, etc. Indentured servants did so voluntarily for a set time and were eventually freed, which was not so for slaves.

Form B:

1. disease
2. governor
3. oath (contract)
4. foe
5. persecute
6. passage
7. apprentice
8. retreat
9. missionary
10. exploration

11. warm, mild, cold, wet, etc.
12. St. Augustine, Fort Duquesne, Fort Necessity, etc.
13. John Smith, Pedro Menendez, Oglethorpe, Penn, etc.
14. teaching, medicine, sales, law, etc.
15. blacksmith, gun smith, watch maker, etc.
16. D
17. A
18. D
19. B
20. The war was fought for control of North America between the French and British. The end of the war meant the end of French influence in the colonies. However, it also meant many casualties and heavy debt for the British.

Form C:

1. contract
2. pewter
3. goods
4. port
5. apprentice
6. service
7. retreat
8. founder
9. missionary
10. foe

11. mercantilism
12. climate
13. marsh
14. class
15. Parliament
16. D
17. A
18. B
19. D
20. Answers may vary but should be well-reasoned.

Skills Forms A-C

21. C
22. B
23. D
24. A
25. C

RESOURCES

www.icw-net.com/tales/mantlost.htm - "The Lost Colony," Tales from the Coast, CoastalGuide by ICW-NET, 2010.

news.yahoo.com/s/ap_travel/20070730/ap_tr_ge/travel_trip_st_augustine - Word, Ron, "St. Augustine: The 'Real' First Settlement in the New World," Associated Press, 2010.

www.foundingfathers.info/us-history/timeline/ - "American Chronology: Timeline for Discovery and Colonization," Founding Fathers. info, Interesting.com, 2010.

www.apva.org/history - "History of Jamestown," APVA.org, The Association for the Preservation of Virginia Antiquities, 2000.

www.tobacco.org/History/Jamestown.html - "A Brief History of Jamestown, Virginia," News and Resources, tobacco.org, 2010.

www.iath.virginia.edu/vcdh/jamestown/rlaws.html - "Laws and Documents Relating to Religion in Early Virginia, 1606-1660," Virtual Jamestown, Crandall Shifflett, 1998.

usinfo.state.gov/usa/infousa/facts/democrac/2.htm - "The Mayflower Compact," Basic Readings in U.S. Democracy, US Information: State Governments, 2010.

www.history.org/history/teaching - Colonial Williamsburg, The Colonial Williamsburg Foundation, 2010.

www.geocities.com/Heartland/Acres/7647/yeoman.htm - "The Yeoman Planters of Colonial Virginia as Recorded on the 1704 Quit Rent Rolls," reprinted from the Planters of Colonial Virginia, 2010.

www.liu.edu/cwis/cwp/library/aaslavry.htm - "A Journey from Slavery to Freedom," The African American, Long Island University, 2010.

www.sjsu.edu/faculty/watkins/coloniallabor.htm - "Colonial Labor," reprinted from Travels Into North America, Pinkerton, 1770.

www.mutualist.org/id64.html - "Mercantilism, Colonialism, and the Creation of the World Market," Mutualist.org, 2010.

www.linksnorth.com/canada-history/french.html - "French and English Rivalry," The History of Canada, linksnorth.com, 2010.

www.ushistory.org/valleyforge/washington/george1.html - "George Washington: The Soldier through the French and Indian War," Historic Valley Forge, Independence Hall Association, 2010.

www.philaprintshop.com/frchintx.html - "A Brief History of the French and Indian War," The Philadelphia Print Shop, Ltd., The Philadelphia Society, 2008.